As a coach with seventeen years' experience, Dr. William E. Warren has a lifetime basketball coaching record of 290 wins and 88 losses. In two full years of coaching track at Toombs Central High School, his teams won the Georgia State Class A Championship once and finished second once. He received two state Coach of the Year awards in girls' track during those years.

Dr. Warren has taught on all levels and has written or co-authored six coaching books including *COACHING AND MOTIVATION*. His articles have appeared in *Scholastic Coach*, *Athletic Journal*, *Coaching Clinic*, *Coach and Athlete*, and *Women's Coaching Clinic*.

COACHING AND WINNING

WILLIAM E. WARREN

PARKER PUBLISHING COMPANY
West Nyack, New York 10995

PRINTED IN THE UNITED STATES OF AMERICA

10 9 8 7 6 5 4 3 2 1

Library of Congress Cataloging-in-Publication Data

Warren, William E.
  Coaching and winning.

  Includes index.
  1. Coaching (Athletics) 2. Motivation (Psychology)
I. Title.
GV711.W35 1987   796′.07′7   87-9225

ISBN 0-13-138983-1

PARKER PUBLISHING COMPANY
BUSINESS & PROFESSIONAL DIVISION
A division of Simon & Schuster
West Nyack, New York 10995

For Louise and Bob
who are winners all the way

I always turn to the sports page first. The sports page records people's accomplishments; the front page has nothing but man's failures.

—Earl Warren

I've always made a total effort, even when the odds seemed entirely against me. I never quit trying; I never felt that I didn't have a chance to win.

—Arnold Palmer

When you win, you're an old pro. When you lose, you're an old man.

—Charley Conerly

INTRODUCTION

Winning—it's the name of the game. We may talk about "victory in defeat" and how losing builds character,* but the bottom line is that all of us coaches want to *win*, or at least to feel like winners. Why, then, do so many of us lose so often?

Part of the answer is obvious. With the exception of tie games (which the optimist counts as half a win and the pessimist would rather forget), every game produces both a winner and a loser. In a ten-team basketball conference that plays a home-and-home double round-robin league schedule, for example, there will be 162 losses up for grabs— along with 162 wins, of course.

In every sport, and in virtually every league or athletic conference, certain teams dominate the upper levels of their league standings year after year. Part of this is easily explained in terms of *winning traditions*. But what is a win-

*A veteran football coach whose team was suffering through the first and only losing season of his career remarked, "This year we're building character— and boy, do I have some characters!"

ning tradition but a continuing state of expecting to win? When athletes operate within an environment in which fans, coaches, and teammates expect them consistently to perform with a high degree of proficiency, they are unlikely to let others down in terms of the physical and mental effort they expend in order to win.

Conversely, when little is expected of players beyond showing up on time, suiting up, and going through the motions of playing the game, they are likely to decide that a total effort toward winning isn't necessary, after all—or worse, they may decide that the game itself isn't important, in which case they are likely to quit playing altogether.

Another aspect of the problem is that certain coaches tend to win more often, and more consistently, than others. Certainly this tendency on the part of some coaches to win and win and win isn't accidental—and it isn't merely a result of a school's having a winning tradition, either. Too many coaches over the years have developed winning programs at more than one school for luck or tradition to be the sole deciding factor in who wins.

The ultimate answers regarding how and why some coaches are able to win consistently while others win occasionally or not at all are to be found in the personality of the coach. While all coaches prefer winning to losing, some coaches will accept no less than a winning effort, whether from their players or from themselves. Such coaches are impelled, by virtue of their extremely competitive nature, toward winning consistently. They find ways to transmit this sense of urgency to their players, supporters, and fans, and as a result they are able to create high expectations toward winning.

But aren't all coaches naturally competitive? Yes, but not to the same extent. Not all coaches are equally affected by losses—it's only a game, remember*—and not all coaches are willing or able to handle the pressure of win-

---

*"Sports is the toy department of human life."—Howard Cosell.

ning consistently, even when such a pattern has been established. Lofty expectations make big-time winning a pressure cooker for coaches—a state that gives real meaning to the term "coaching burnout."

Also, not all coaches demand a total effort from their players, and not all are totally committed to giving the kind of effort that is necessary to build a winning program. Some coaches simply are not intense enough in their work habits and approach to the game to attract and keep players in their program who will want to win for them.

You can be a winner in your coaching—and you *will* be—if you believe in yourself, and if you have unswerving devotion to a dream of what you can achieve in coaching. Through the example of your own performance and expectations, you will attract players into your program who accept your values and share your dream of what can be accomplished through hard work, commitment, and dedication.

It won't be easy—few things of lasting value in life are accomplished easily and without great sacrifice—but it can be done. Every year, and on every level of play, thousands of coaches find ways to instill in their players the desire to become more than they were, through hard work and commitment to team goals.

My primary reason for writing this book on the dynamics of winning has been to impart to you the good news that you have within yourself the seeds of greatness. *You can be as good a coach as you want to be.* If you believe this statement (and there is no reason why you shouldn't, unless you also believe that great coaches such as basketball's John Wooden and football's Paul "Bear" Bryant became great by virtue of their reputations rather than by hard work) you should be able to convince your players that they too are capable of great achievement, both individually and collectively, through dedication and hard work.

The ability to win, and to win consistently, does not involve magical powers or dark, mystical secrets shared by a select few. It is not a matter of superhuman coaches whose knowledge, insights, and coaching ability are beyond the comprehension of mere mortals. It is, rather, an orderly, predictable process that begins with a coach who, for whatever reason, makes the conscious decision that he or she absolutely will *not* accept the inevitability of losing as a way of life.

If you have not already done so, I urge you to make that decision today.

You'll never regret it.

CONTENTS

LEARNING TO WIN OR TO LOSE— AN ACQUIRED TRAIT

chapter **1**

The taste of defeat has a richness of experience all its own.

—*Bill Bradley*

[Coach Knute] Rockne wanted nothing but "bad losers." Good losers get into the habit of losing.

—*George Allen*

When I began my basketball coaching career at Jane Macon Junior High School in Brunswick, Georgia, in January, 1964, it never dawned on me that I might have to teach people how to win. In my youthful ignorance, I naively assumed that, because athletes want to win, they also know *how* to win. (As a matter of fact, we won 16 of 20 games while I was at the school, but it probably wasn't *my* fault: at that tender stage of my coaching development, I couldn't have taught a fish to swim.)

I can see now how lucky I was to have had fine athletes to carry me through that initial learning period; I was able to learn from my mistakes without undergoing any kind of prolonged losing period that might have driven me prematurely out of coaching. It was only later, after a number of years of coaching winning teams, that I had to confront the other side of the coin—players who understood and accepted losing as a way of life.

THE EMERGING SELF

All living is learning. From the very moment of birth, we begin to learn about ourselves and our relation to our environment. Unfortunately, much of this learning is painful, because life itself is often painful and traumatic.

In his excellent textbook, *Health: Man in a Changing Environment*,* Dr. Benjamin Kogan eloquently describes

---

*Kogan, Benjamin A. *Health: Man in a Changing Environment*. New York: Harcourt, Brace & World, Inc., 1970.

the process of the harsh and sudden transition of an infant from an aquatic existence, a comfortable, warm, watery life within the womb, to that of a terrestrial, air-breathing being, thrust into a world not of the child's own choosing or making. And if the newborn child is not crying at birth, Dr. Kogan asserts—if he is not already aware of the painful nature of life outside the womb—the doctor spanks him until he cries.

The sometimes painful process of discovering who and what we are continues throughout our lives. Gradually, we acquire personalities, or *selves*, that are uniquely our own, for better or worse. For teenagers, the struggle toward selfhood is particularly acute because, in many cases, they are too inexperienced to deal with the complexities of four conflicting facets of their emerging personalities: the person they *are*; the person they *think* they are (or want to be); the person they want others to think they are; and the person others think they are.

The natural outgrowth of this state of lingering uncertainty is, understandably, confusion on the part of the teenager. The teacher or coach who fails to take into account this confused state in dealing with young people is unlikely to achieve any kind of meaningful, lasting, two-way communication with them.

Thus, we begin with a problem of goals: while we as coaches may be concerned primarily with winning—as Vince Lombardi declared, "If you aren't fired with *enthusiasm*, you will be *fired* with enthusiasm"—the youngsters who are playing for us may have what they perceive to be weightier problems facing them, namely, learning about themselves in order to learn to face life responsibly as adults. Many's the coach who has remarked at the frustration of placing his coaching career in the hands of a 16- or 17-year old athlete who happens to run the 100 in 9.4 or throw a football 65 yards on the run—when he's not having squabbles with his parents or spats with his girlfriend.

Still, it must be faced as any occupational hazard must be confronted, since the alternative is to find another, less threatening line of work, such as selling senior rings or sporting goods.

Coping with a Negative Self-Image

As was pointed out previously, everything in life is learned—and this includes our concepts of the importance of winning and losing. Indeed, much of our personalities derive from the basic view of ourselves as winners or losers. The youngsters we coach have already formed elementary judgments about themselves in this regard, and often their self-assessments are highly negative. Even as they are struggling to attain adult status, they continue to be treated as children by their parents, teachers, and other adults (including coaches), who expect them to be obedient and follow orders. And while there's nothing wrong with obedience per se (one can hardly expect to achieve success in life (or in sports) without having learned to follow orders somewhere along the way) youngsters are fed an endless diet of commands to be obeyed from the moment when, as toddlers taking their first steps, they hear Mom or Dad's first "no!" when they reach for a breakable object on the coffee table. Eventually they become conditioned to the idea that whatever they do is subject to adult approval. That's why we so often hear children grumble, "Everything I do is wrong," and that's at least part of the reason why in so many cases their self-concepts are negative. They are confused and discouraged as to who they want to be as opposed to who adults will let them be.

This is, of course, what growing up is all about. Still, negativity is basically destructive, at least when applied to immature youngsters who are stumbling and fumbling their way toward adulthood. Among the many coaching tasks facing us is to reinforce in our young athletes' minds the notion that being a part of a team will help to make them winners in life, if not in every game along the way.

We simply cannot allow those youngsters on our teams who have a negative self-image to continue to believe that they are not basically worthwhile individuals. We are not merely cheating them if we ignore their need for acceptance and guidance, we are cheating ourselves and our teams as well, in terms of the performances such players might be able to give once they begin to view themselves in a more positive light.

Put more simply, our players are unlikely to achieve any kind of lasting, positive results in their sports participation as long as they perceive themselves in negative terms or consider their contributions to the team's success to be minimal.

Changing the "Loser" Image

At best, losing is a humbling experience; at worst—say, a prolonged losing streak—it can become a cancer that erodes team morale and reinforces in some players' minds the notion that they are losers. Concerning the latter, continued negative results usually lead to negative expectations for future successes, and thereby increase the chances of failure in the future.

Still, it doesn't have to be that way. Somewhere along the way during our years of coaching, it dawns on most of us that we are smarter than most of the teenagers we coach. And while such a revelation may not appear earthshaking, it should lead us to the conclusion that, even in a losing situation, we can direct our players' attention away from short-term failures (for example, today's loss), and toward long-term success; that is, toward a winning program in the future.

The player who sees himself as a loser doesn't need to undergo a losing streak to be reminded of his shortcomings; he is already painfully aware of them. What he needs is to be reminded of his *successes*, however minimal they may be. "Small strokes fell great oaks," or so the saying goes; changing a negative self-image almost always involves small strokes, and small successes.

If our team is losing consistently, the intensity level of

our players' performances is likely to begin to tail off at some point as the losses continue to pile up. Shouting at them, threatening them, or punishing them isn't likely to work, because as *losers* they may expect to be treated accordingly. Too, such behavior on our part may force them to the ultimate decision, that of quitting our team. That way, at least, they won't lose any more games, and they won't be shouted at, threatened, or punished.

THREE STEPS TO ALTERING PLAYERS' SELF-IMAGES AS LOSERS

The solution to the problem of overcoming players' self-concepts as "losers" is three-fold. Here's how it works.

Step 1:   Define Goals Carefully

The coach must carefully define individual and team goals which, while realistic, are challenging enough to require that the players extend themselves beyond their present level of skills and effort.   He should set realistic short-term goals (which may or may not include winning—that's *his* goal, but it doesn't have to be his stated goal for his players), and at the same time he should describe his long-range goals (which usually include, but should not be confined to, winning.)

Concerning short-term goals, it is especially important to emphasize *improvement*, not winning, whenever the team is likely to lose. In fact, many highly successful coaches *never* mention winning to their players except in terms of long-range goals.

At the same time, the coach's short-term goal—unstated, of course—is to gradually raise the level of expectations in terms of individual and team progress. As short-term goals are achieved, the coach should both identify those successes and formulate new and challenging short-term goals for the team. (His long-range goal—building a consistently winning program—remains constant until it becomes a matter of maintaining a consistently winning program, followed by building and maintaining a *championship* program.)

Whenever a coach suddenly expects more from his players and the team than he did previously, he automatically increases the amount of anxiety they feel, both individually and collectively. Building a consistent winner requires training players to handle the pressure associated with winning the close games. In a losing situation, the coach must be aware that, if his expectations are raised too high or too quickly, the resulting anxiety (or stress, or pressure, or whatever term you prefer) will be counterproductive to his program-building efforts, at least on a short-term basis.

Still, it cannot be emphasized too strongly that *program growth cannot occur in the absence of controlled anxiety.* If players are not exposed regularly in daily practice to stressful situations that require them to exert themselves physically or mentally beyond the level at which they operate comfortably right now—their so-called "comfort zone"—they will not continue to improve, and they will not learn to perform skills correctly under the stressful conditions of actual games.

Long-range goals should not be too specific or too hasty, unless the players are either highly skilled or improving rapidly. Dynasties are not built in a day, or even in a single season. If we tell our players that three weeks from now we'll be winning every game, we'd better have a sound basis for making such a judgment or we may stand to lose much of our credibility with our players. And in coaching, credibility is everything. That's why our short-term goals, at least, should be realistic.

Setting and pursuing goals provides structure in our lives by directing and focusing our attention and our energies in desirable, predetermined channels. Too, the act of setting goals provides us with a basis for comparing players' performances with the expectations that we have set for them.

Step 2: Show Faith in Your Players' Abilities

The coach must constantly express his confidence and faith in his players' abilities to pursue and achieve the short- and long-term expectations he has outlined for them in terms of individual and team goals. Regardless of how the season is going, the coach must never, under any circumstances, display a lack of faith in his players' ability to show progress, either individually or as a team. He may show displeasure at their performances on a game-to-game basis, but not to the extent of letting them know that he has given up on them. If that happens, he has lost more than just another battle; he's lost the war, because he'll never reach those players again.

Step 3: Offer Opportunities to Achieve Success

The coach must provide his players with opportunities to achieve success, however slight, and with immediate feedback in terms of recognition and approval whenever they achieve positive results. He may have to work diligently to find signs of individual and team progress, but it can and must be done.* Players must be shown that their hard work is paying off, or they will not continue to work hard. They must be convinced that they are progressing, however marginally, toward the ultimate achievement of team goals. *Progress* and *achievement* are positive evidence that both our goals and the players who are pursuing them are worthwhile. (In fairness, I must point out that not every coach agrees with or accepts the notion that players who are used to losing can be taught to play as winners. Alabama's Bear Bryant seldom recruited high school players from losing teams; he preferred athletes whose backgrounds were firmly rooted in winning traditions.)

---

*Regarding statistics, one coach told me, "Give me the figures, and I'll find a way to convince you that the Germans actually won World War II!"

THE COACH AS A TEACHER

In a very real sense, all effective coaching is effective teaching. It follows, then, that every good coach is a good teacher.

Obviously, the coach who hopes to win regularly must be able to teach the skills and strategies associated with his sport; he cannot realistically expect his players to acquire those skills on their own without benefit of instruction. It should be equally apparent that, as the coach's understanding of the finer points of the game and coaching broadens, he will be able to impart increasingly complex and sophisticated concepts, skills, and strategies to his players. There's more to it than that, however.

In coaching, teaching involves far more than diagramming plays and demonstrating skills. Virtually every action undertaken by the coach teaches. A smile or a friendly pat on the back teaches, as does a frown. They teach acceptance or rejection, satisfaction or dissatisfaction. Sometimes such gestures communicate far more than words could ever say. They teach players how others see them, and they reinforce or contradict previously established self-images as winners or losers.

Thus, it becomes apparent that, since self-concept is unique to each individual, the motivational needs of players on our teams will vary considerably. An approach to motivation directed at the team as a whole usually is less effective than an individualized approach would be when combined with team motivational efforts. Some players respond best to prodding (pushing), while others need encouragement (pulling); the phrase "different strokes for different folks" applies here. The success of our teaching may depend to a great extent upon our awareness of which players need which type of motivating, when they need it, and how it shall be applied.

If the effective coach is also an effective teacher, it is equally true that he is an effective psychologist: he knows his players well enough to understand their motivational needs; that is, what it takes to motivate them toward peak performances, and he takes those needs into account whenever possible in dealing with them.*

Four Principles for Teaching Players How to Win

1. **It is easier to learn how to lose than to learn how to win.** Jockey Willie Shoemaker probably said it best: "There are 199 ways to get beat, but only one way to win—get there (to the finish line) first!"

Learning to lose consistently in sports is easy to do, and surprisingly so, considering that the vast majority of players and coaches would rather win than lose.

Losing requires no coaching experience or expertise, no inspirational speeches, no special game plans or preparations; in fact, all we have to do in most cases is sit back and wait for nature to take its course. Even the weakest of opponents usually will find a way to beat us if we give them enough opportunities. If we repeat that process game after game until we're comfortable with it, we'll soon find losses piling up faster than the national debt.

Having overcome our natural desire to win and mastered the art of snatching defeat from the jaws of victory, we are likely to discover that losing isn't as bad as people say it is. After all, there's no pressure on us to win when everyone expects us to lose; and then, when we lose as expected, we haven't disappointed anyone. Our families still love us, and our enemies still hate us. Life goes on as usual. Losing still may hurt to a certain extent, but not as much as it would if we expected to win.

Losing consistently is like being born ugly: you're reminded of it every now and then, but eventually you get used to it. After awhile, you hardly notice it anymore.

---

*For a broader, more detailed analysis of motivation in theory and practice, the reader is referred to the author's book, *Coaching and Motivation* (Englewood Cliffs, N.J.: Prentice-Hall, Inc., 1983.)

Besides, we can always find excuses or alibis if we need them. History has given us a rich and colorful legacy of excuses for every occasion, ranging from the student's "The dog ate my homework!" to the athlete's "I could have won if I'd *wanted* to!" or "We wuz robbed!"

We don't have to teach people how to lose. Like learning how to use profanity, losing comes naturally to many people. Rather, what we need to do is to teach our players how *not* to lose.

2.   In losing situations, players must be taught why winning is important.   It is not enough to assume that our players already appreciate the values of winning in their lives. As we have seen, many youngsters come to us with perceptions of themselves as losers. Before we can begin to win consistently with such players, we must use every means at our disposal to build within them a sense of pride in workmanship and accomplishment.

Team pride is the foundation of every successful athletic program. Winning builds pride, but so do hard work and commitment to team goals, even in coaching situations where successes are measured by the tablespoonful rather than by the gallon.

3.   Players must be taught not to accept the inevitability of defeat.   If we intend to alter losing attitudes, we must first show by our own actions that we will not accept losing as inevitable. Everyone loses at least occasionally; still, we cannot coach as if we *expect* to lose, or as if even occasional defeats mean nothing to us. We should not expect our players to take defeats seriously unless *we* take them seriously.

In my third year of coaching girls' basketball at Toombs Central High School, I had a group of very short, very inexperienced girls returning from the previous year's highly successful team, which won 25 games and lost only two. We won our first two games that third season with two juniors and three freshmen in the lineup (none of whom was taller than 5'4"). Then we proceeded to lose our next four games.

Visions of suicide began to dance through my head: I had never before lost more than four games in a season.

Meanwhile, our new boys' basketball coach, who had played four years of college basketball prior to entering coaching several years before, was struggling with the remnants of a team that had gone 16–10 the previous season. While it was painfully obvious (to me, at least) that both teams were suffering the growing pains of a rebuilding season, the boys' coach always seemed to shrug off the effects of his team's mounting losses within ten minutes of the final buzzer.

We'd get on the bus for the long ride home from another disappointing road loss, wrung out, discouraged, and disheartened, looking for reassurance from each other that it wasn't the end of the world. Inevitably, the boys' coach would sit down, look at me and say, "Dawggone, Bill, I just don't *know* what's the matter! We *lose* and we *lose*. It reminds me of when I was at (a certain college), and we were playing Florida State in Tallahassee, and I had to guard Dave Cowens. Well, he was six-eight and I was only six-four, but I weighed about two-thirty, so what I had to do was lean on him, and. . . ." And off he'd go, reliving the high points of his basketball playing days while I was agonizing inside about how to change our losing ways by drawing gallons of skills from pint jars of talent.

To make a long story longer, starting with our seventh game my freshmen finally began to realize that it was possible for them to chew gum, run, and think at the same time, and we won 12 of our next 15 games. Our final record of 14–9 was less than spectacular, admittedly, but at least it showed glimmers of hope for the future (which were borne out by subsequent 17–6 and 20–3 seasons as those tiny freshmen matured).

The boys, on the other hand, reversed our records with 9–14, 6–15, and 3–18 seasons—and their downhill slide all began with a coach who preferred not to worry about why his team was losing.

A second method by which a coach can teach players

not to accept defeat as inevitable is to give them real opportunities to win, or at least to compete as equals until they
begin to accept the possibility of winning as real for them.
In some cases, this means scheduling wisely and creatively
to include a number of teams that you have a realistic
chance of defeating.

Let's face it: losing may teach us many things about
ourselves, both good and bad, but losing consistently does
nothing to teach us how to win. The best way to learn how
to win consistently is to *win*, and to keep on winning until a
habit of winning expectations is established.

An incredible coaching feat occurred recently at
Woody Gap High School in the tiny unincorporated north
Georgia town of Suches: a good friend of mine, John
Alexander, led his girls' basketball team to a 12–10 record.

What's so incredible about that, you ask. Well, for starters, it was Coach Alexander's first year at the school, and
the girls' team had won only nine games in the past two
years. More importantly, though, Woody Gap is one of only
three schools remaining in the state of Georgia that has
grades K–12 within the same school. The average daily attendance for all 13 grades at Woody Gap was only 117, with
grades 9 through 12 accounting for 28 of those students.
And since half of that total was boys, there were a total of 14
girls in Woody Gap High School.

Coach Alexander began the season with eight players
(or 57 percent of the high school's female population) on his
girls' team, but one girl quit after a couple of games and another was injured and missed the last half of the season.
Still, he somehow managed to win 12 games, largely with a
squad of six players, none of whom was experienced in winning previously.

How did he do it? When Coach Alexander arrived at
the school in June, he discovered that the previous coach
had scheduled only three games for the following basketball
season. Instead of following past procedures and
completing the schedule by adding larger schools that

Woody Gap could not possibly compete with, he turned to the section of the GHSA Handbook that listed the average daily attendance of all Georgia high schools, searched for those in his general area of the state that were comparable in size to Woody Gap, and contacted those coaches about scheduling home-and-home games with them. He also scheduled games with a small high school in North Carolina, and added enough regular-season games with larger regional opponents to complete his schedule.

Six of his team's ten losses came at the hands of schools at least five times as large as Woody Gap. Thus, while Coach Alexander was teaching skills that would lead to winning, he also was giving his team a realistic chance to win at least some of the time, by virture of creative scheduling.

There's nothing in the rule book that says that, because we've entered a losing situation, we have to roll over and play dead just because other schools who are used to pounding our team senseless would like to continue to do so at our expense. And if competitive scheduling can improve our team's chances for success, I for one believe that we owe ourselves and our teams that opportunity. As skills and confidence increase, then we can increase the competitiveness of our schedule to provide greater challenges for our team.

I used creative scheduling to reverse a three-year 12–57 record in girls' basketball at Toombs Central (whose average daily attendance, incidentally, was 114) to 25–2 in only two years. We weren't that good, of course—but if my players wanted to believe otherwise, I wasn't going to argue the point with them. As their confidence grew, so did their skills and the level of intensity of their performance, both in practices and in games.

Incidentally, I spoke at Woody Gap's sports banquet recently. It was held in the lunchroom, and seldom have I encountered a more enthusiastic group of athletes at any level of play. After the banquet, Coach Alexander noticed that the lights had been turned on in the gym, and when we went to investigate we found his girls shooting baskets in their dresses or slacks and stocking feet.

They understand exactly what world champion skier Jean-Claude Killy meant when he said, "Winning tastes good." They've had a taste of success and winning, and they like it.

If I were a betting man, I'd bet that Coach Alexander and the girls of Woody Gap High School (average daily attendance: 28) will win considerably more than 12 games next year.*

4. Players must be taught how to give a winning effort, win or lose.   In many cases, especially those in which players are used to losing, two problems are likely to crop up: (a) the players may not understand that winning requires a 100 percent effort, or else they may think that they're giving 100 percent when in fact they are playing at half-effort or less; and (b) because they have already established (incorrectly) in their own minds what constitutes a total effort for them, they may be unwilling to give any kind of sustained greater effort just because *we* say it will improve the team's chances of winning.

Regarding Point (a), many players—and surprisingly, many coaches as well—fail to realize that often a very fine line exists between winning and losing. Former L.A. Rams great Merlin Olsen declared, "You take the best team and the worst team (in the NFL) and line them up and you would find very little physical difference. You would find an emotional difference. The winning team has a dedication ... they will not accept defeat." And regarding Point (b), these players—the ones who will work only at their own previously established levels of performance—are the ones who are likely to quit when we try to raise the team's level of conditioning, hustle, and general intensity of play. Or worse, they won't quit, but will stay with the team like a fes-

---

*Their record the next season was 17–5. —Ed.

tering sore that won't heal, griping and causing unrest and agitation, until you find yourself counting the days and hours until they graduate.

HOW TO PROMOTE A WINNING EFFORT

Prepare Your Players to Win

A winning effort begins with *preparing* to win. This, in turn, begins with the rigorous physical conditioning players must undergo in order to play hard without letup or undue fatigue for as long as necessary in a game.* As one coach said, "It's all right to lose now and then—but not because your team was out of shape to win!"

Rigorous conditioning is never wasted, because it builds pride as well as strength and endurance. Players may object to our conditioning program initially (and in a losing program, some players may quit the team rather than undergo intense conditioning drills) but it must be done. Eventually, the players who stay with us will realize that hard work is not fatal, and we can actually use our conditioning program as a source of pride in accomplishment in the same manner that marine recruits boast of having survived their basic training at Parris Island.

The key here is communication. If we merely drive our players constantly when they aren't used to that kind of intensity, they're likely to quit on us. But if we constantly stress that *We have to work harder than our opponents are working if we want to catch up with them,* and remind them at every opportunity that their hard work will pay off sooner or later—that is, if we keep their attention focused on our long-range goals rather than the pain they're undergoing right now—most of our players will stay with us, if for no other reason than to see whether we're telling the truth or talking through our hat. And when our team later wins

---

*"Fatigue makes cowards of us all." —Vince Lombardi

games because opponents aren't in shape to beat us in the latter stages of games, it offers conclusive evidence that our approach to conditioning is working, and that our players' hard work has not been done in vain.

Strenuous physical conditioning does not always win games, of course; few problems in life are ever resolved that simply. But you can bet your last dollar that a lack of conditioning will lose games—again, not always, but often enough to make it apparent that training harder might have changed the outcomes of those games.

Promote the Idea That Hard Work Pays Off

Along with physical conditioning, preparing to win also refers to instilling in our players the belief that *hard work pays off*, and the harder they work, the more they will achieve. While the truth of this statement may appear to be self-evident, it isn't, not by a long shot. When players are used to losing, the only obvious feature of competition as they see it is that they're going to continue to lose, no matter how hard they try.

As we push, pull, and otherwise drive our teams toward ever-increasing levels of physical and mental toughness, we must also be careful to remind them constantly of why they're working so hard, and search for ways to show them that hard work is improving the caliber of their play. In losing situations, this translates into motivating them to achieve through hard work what they failed to achieve previously.

Help Your Players Realize Their Full Potential

Another aspect of teaching players what constitutes a winning effort is that they cannot be permitted to give less than what *we*, their coaches, believe to be a total effort for them. Players must not be allowed to decide for themselves when they will hustle and when they will not.

Players don't know what they're capable of achieving, whether individually or as a team. They have neither the maturity nor the self-understanding to realistically assess their athletic potential, nor to determine with any degree of accuracy the extent to which they are working toward the realization of that potential.

That's our job, as coaches. We assess athletic potential and we try to find ways to develop that potential to the fullest extent possible. And since full potential is never derived from half-efforts, it makes no sense for us to turn over to our players the choices of when and how hard they will work.

To draw a parallel from another area, how successful is a business likely to be if the boss permits his employees to work only as hard or as long as they feel like working? And why should leadership in business be any different from leadership in coaching? After all, the company is a team, pursuing team goals. The company's economic success or failure will be determined largely by the amount and quality of work performed by its employees. As O. J. Simpson said in the Hertz Rent-a-Car advertisements, "We're number two, so we try harder."

Teach Players to Concentrate

A third aspect of winning efforts is that of teaching players to concentrate.

As Rudyard Kipling wrote: "If you can keep your head while all about you are losing theirs. . . ." Echoing this sentiment, the old coaching adage that "games aren't won; they're lost," refers in large part to lapses in concentration that occur at inopportune moments. Many coaches will tell you that, in the majority of cases, it's not spectacular last-second, game-saving plays that win games, but rather untimely, critical mistakes which *lose* games, made by players who probably should have known better.

While it is true that to err is human, it is also true that people who concentrate on what they're doing make fewer mistakes than those who allow their concentration to waver. For example, less than 1 percent of the nation's vehicular accidents are due to mechanical malfunctions; the other 99-plus percent are due to driver error of some kind. And accident proneness appears to be more than anything else a result of habitual lapses in judgment and/or concentration.

Concentration is taught through the use of drills that require players to think about what they're doing and to do it correctly. Because the ability to concentrate is both a learned trait and a habit, players can be taught to increase the intensity as well as the duration of their concentration through the use of carefully selected drills and a system of rewards and punishment.

Although the opposite may appear to be true, drills that simulate game situations are superior to scrimmaging under full-scale game conditions as a means of improving concentration—at least in terms of the level of attention required of the players. In drills, players practice the same skills repeatedly in a confined area, and mistakes are quickly identified and corrected. In scrimmaging, however, mistakes often go unnoticed or overlooked, and the players' concentration is divided among a vastly broader range of skills and playing strategies. (This is not to say, of course, that scrimmaging should never be used; rather, we're saying that drills, and not scrimmaging, should be used to teach and practice skills, and to correct mistakes.) Before players are taught to concentrate for long periods of time, they should first be taught to concentrate intensely for short periods of time within specific, controlled areas of the game such as those provided by drills.

Admittedly, the task of improving concentration is difficult in this day and age in which television has shortened attention spans to 30-second segments; still, the effort to increase and prolong our players' concentration is a vital factor in teaching players to give their best effort mentally as well as physically.

HOW TO CONTROL PLAYERS' INTENSITY

Teaching players to concentrate is, in a very real sense, teaching them to give 100 percent mentally to the task at hand. But players must also be taught how to concentrate while giving an all-out effort physically. Taken together (because they cannot realistically be separated), these aspects of performance comprise what we refer to as "playing with intensity." But because we expect players to concentrate while they are going all-out physically—a far more difficult task than performing either activity to the exclusion of the other—what we are really talking about here might more properly be termed "playing with *controlled* intensity."

Can young athletes be taught to play with controlled intensity? Of course they can. It's simply a matter of psychological conditioning that begins with the first second of preseason practice. If we carefully expose our athletes to a highly organized, highly disciplined program of daily activities in which they are constantly encouraged by every means available to respond in an intense manner, eventually they will become conditioned to respond intensely in all competitive athletic situations. Sometimes the conditioning comes abruptly, sometimes it is a gradual process. But whenever it arrives, the end result—players who allow us as coaches to decide for them the level of intensity that is acceptable for them in given situations—is well worth the wait. It is a vital key to effective coaching.

Five Guidelines for Building Intensity

The following principles and guidelines exist which may assist us in understanding, and thus hastening, the conditioning process:

1.   **Intensity, like laziness, is a learned trait, a habit.** And because it is a very good habit for athletes (and coaches) to adopt, it should be stressed and emphasized constantly.

2. Communication is the key to teaching.   Everything we do or say communicates. Concerning verbal communication, it is important to define terms precisely, often,
early, and in as many ways as necessary to make yourselves
understood. The last day of the season is not the time to explain to the players what we meant by "*playing hard.*"

Concerning visual communication, it is important to
remember that our enthusiasm and love for our sport shows
in our faces and our body language. Unfortunately, so does
our indecision, lack of preparedness, or lack of interest in
the sport. You can talk all you want about "giving 100 percent," but you'd better believe that, after watching you in
action for a couple of weeks, every kid on your squad will
know whether you're really as committed to winning as you
say you are.

3. Begin as early as possible to build intensity.
When building intensity, start as early as possible. In one
sense, this refers to expectations—those of the coach versus
those of the individual players—and whose expectations
shall prevail. If we let the players decide when they will
hustle or concentrate and when they will not, we should not
be surprised or disappointed to find them slacking off at inopportune moments—say, when games are on the line and
waiting to be won by the team that gives the better effort.

When we set high expectations initially, our players
will test us to find out if we really mean what we say. And
when we follow through in our demands for a total effort by
rewarding positive efforts and punishing half-hearted or
lackadaisical performances—well, they'll get the picture
sooner or later (probably *sooner*). When they realize that
their alternatives have been reduced to only two choices—
giving a total effort whenever we say to, or quitting the
team—the true athletes will do as we ask, and the fakers will
quit, and in both cases the team will be better off.

If, on the other hand, we set low expectations initially
regarding the level of intensity we will accept, or if we fail
to set any level of performance intensity at all in the early

stages of preseason practice, our players will never have to test us at all. They'll know from the start that they can do as they please.

4. Daily practice sessions are the heart and soul of the coaching process.   Teams that do not regularly practice with intensity seldom play with intensity. Anyone who tells you otherwise is selling you a bill of goods.

5. The same principle applies to players. Sure you're going to treat your superstars differently—you can't help it, because they *are* different*—but you can use that difference to your advantage. Instead of simply allowing the gifted players to do as they please at practice, you should be prepared to spend considerable time with them away from the court or playing field, talking with him or her about such things as responsibilities to the team and to one's teammates, becoming a more complete player by working hard to improve areas of individual weakness, and your belief in the biblical dictum that "To whom much is given, much shall be required, and of him to whom much has been entrusted, people will demand the more."

At any rate, your private talks with these players should be directed toward making them feel a sense of obligation toward you, the team, and the school rather than the other way around. They as well as you should bear in mind that successful programs do not become that way simply through the presence of superstar players; rather, they are the predictable result of coaches and players who, united in their determination not to lose or accept less than their best performances, have dedicated themselves to the pursuit of victory and individual and team excellence.

------

*If you dispute this point, wait until the next time your superstar linebacker (who bench presses 455 pounds and runs a 4.4 forty) twists an ankle in practice. If you can treat his injury the same as a similar injury to your 130-pound freshman guard who benches 195 and runs the forty in 5.4—if you can keep a Tom Landry face while your superstar is lying on the ground, writhing in pain—well, you're a better man than I.

In any event, the bottom line for me has always been communicating to all the players on my teams that, regardless of their skills and ability, they must earn their place in the starting lineup—and their subsequent playing time as well—by the intensity level of their practices. I'll play anyone and everyone on the squad who'll give me the proverbial 110 percent, day in and day out, at practice and in games, and my players know it. They know that giving a total effort is more important to me than winning games, and as a result our games and practice sessions usually are rather spirited, to put it mildly. I can't imagine how many times over the years I've told players on my teams: "I play favorites on this team, and my favorites are the ones who bust their buns every day, giving it all they've got whether they feel like it or not."

Don't Swallow the Myth About Tough Practice Workouts

Before leaving the topic of intensity, I'd like to discuss briefly a coaching myth that has arisen in recent years; namely, if your practice workouts are too hard or too intense, your kids are more likely to get hurt. In fact, exactly the opposite is true. Half-efforts are a far more prevalent cause of athletic injuries.

For example, a football offensive lineman makes his block; then, assuming incorrectly that the play is over as far as he is concerned, he relaxes and stands up to watch the play, only to be blind-sided by an overzealous defender. The ref throws a flag on the defender, but *we're* the ones who are really penalized, because for the time being we've lost a starting lineman to injury. Or an opponent is driving the baseline in basketball, and rather than sliding all the way over to cut him off and take the charge head-on, our defender simply leans toward the dribbler. When the inevitable contact occurs, our player is knocked off balance, falls, and suffers a separated shoulder. In both cases, the injury might have been avoided if our player had given a total effort on the play, both physically and mentally.

Coaches who tell you that intense practices are needlessly dangerous are merely trying to justify the fact that their own practices are easy. As Jerry Tarkanian of the University of Nevada at Las Vegas told me once, "All practices should be intense. We never have *easy* practices—but sometimes we have *shorter* practices."

SIX POINTS TO KEEP IN MIND WHEN YOU ARE ENTERING A WINNING SITUATION

In my earlier book on motivation, I devoted considerable attention to the problems associated with entering a losing situation; I did not, however, devote similar attention to the converse of that situation; namely, assuming a coaching position in a program that already is successful. This oversight resulted from my assumption that anyone who can build a winning program where none existed previously is capable of doing at least as well in a program where winning has become traditional. Still, that assumption did nothing to help the coach who faces such a situation. *All* coaching situations have unique problems that must be faced and dealt with, and just because those problems involve maintaining a winning tradition does not mean that they are any less acute, or that they require less than 100 percent of a coach's attention, patience, and perseverance in searching for solutions.

Guidelines, principles, and points to consider when entering a winning situation might include the following:

1. The more consistently a team has won in the past, the less likely its fans and boosters will be to accept losing, and the shorter will be the "grace period" granted the new coach while he establishes his own program and identity. If, for example, you're entering a losing situation, you usually can find ways to convince the people around you that you can build a winning program in three or four years. In a winning situation, though, people are more likely to want to see those wins right now. They are less likely to be forgiving concerning losses along the way, and more likely to effect the dismissal of any coach who cannot win often enough to suit them.

No one, it seems, is immune to the wrath of fans who have become spoiled by their team's successes. When UCLA's John Wooden retired after having won ten NCAA basketball titles in his last 12 years of coaching, you had to feel sorry for his successor, Gene Bartow. A soft-spoken, brilliant tactician who guided his Memphis State Tigers to the national finals in 1973 before bowing to Wooden's UCLA Bruins, 87–66, Bartow's winning percentage at UCLA actually was *higher* than Wooden's had been. But Bartow failed to win a national title in either of his two years at the school. He eventually resigned, unable to withstand the awesome pressures involved in following a coaching legend. At this writing, he is still winning big, presently at the University of Alabama at Birmingham.

2. Don't try to be a carbon copy of the previous coach. Unless you're his or her identical twin, you aren't a carbon copy anyway, so why try to be someone you're not? You're better off being yourself, for better or worse, and spending your time trying to communicate your own virtues, values, and goals rather than wasting everyone's time with a charade that isn't going to work anyway.

Along with this, you should be prepared to deal with people who expect you to win the same way that the previous coach won, which may or may not be realistic in your particular situation.

No matter what you do, you aren't going to satisfy everyone. Even if you win every game, there'll be parents in the stands who think that their sons or daughters should have received more playing time, or that your coaching strategy or the team's style of play stinks to high heaven, simply because it's different from what they're used to. In time they'll get used to your methods and philosophy—if you win often enough to keep them from running you off.

3. Don't make drastic changes in the program unless you're absolutely certain that drastic changes are necessary. Sometimes the need for drastic changes may be clearly indicated; for example, when you inherit a very young, very inexperienced squad that cannot grasp the intricacies of the complex offenses or defenses used by the previous year's senior-laden squad. In such cases, the coach who must win immediately in order to retain his job may be impelled toward making rather drastic changes in playing style. For another example, the coach may pursue a different philosophy from the previous coach (e.g., defense-oriented rather than offense-oriented), in which case he would naturally bring changes and a new look to the team's playing style.

What we're saying here, though, is that *the coach should not make changes simply for the sake of change*, and *in the beginning his changes should be as minor as possible*—with the exception of situations in which the coach has ample time to effect his changes without adversely affecting the players' performances. But two factors should be borne in mind here: first, the team already was successful using its previous playing style; and second, the farther the team strays from what it knows best, the more mistakes it will make until the players absorb and accept the new style of play. A brief example should suffice to determine why this should be so.

Let's say that I'm basically an advocate of run-and-shoot football. Let's say too that my new school has had great success in recent years operating a ball-control-oriented power running attack. In making an abrupt, wholesale switch from the proven style of play that the players already know and have confidence in, I'm making their job more difficult initially in two ways: I'm exposing them to unknowns (including myself and my philosophy), which they do not yet understand or believe in, and I'm forcing them to learn new techniques which, in some cases (for example, pass blocking versus run blocking), are radically different from what they are used to. They may, of course, continue to win despite the changes, but on the other hand they may *not* win, at least in the beginning, in which case their confidence in me *and* the playing style I forced upon them will suffer, and will make my job more difficult for a while.

It's all a matter of the coach's feel for the situation and what his players can absorb and learn at one time. In my own case, I would prefer to fit myself into the winning situation rather than bending it radically to accommodate me. I like the idea of coming into the winning situation and building gradually upon what the players already know. (It's not a bad idea in entering a *losing* situation, either.) I prefer to make the players' job as easy as possible while they're getting used to me and learning what I stand for. For me that means making minor adjustments and modifications in their playing style—where it conflicts with my own preferences, that is—and doing so in such a gradual manner that the players are not intimidated or bothered by them. I'd rather not run the risk of upsetting the rhythm and intensity of their play by the wholesale adoption of a style of play that is totally alien to what they already know, if I can avoid such a pitfall.

Of course, some coaches, especially in football where styles of play vary widely, prefer to go whole hog and make all of their changes in one fell swoop—and that's all right, too, *if the players are capable of learning all that must be learned in the time available.* In order for players to operate effectively in a new playing style, though, they must be familiar enough with it to act without having to pause and think about what they're doing; otherwise, their aggressiveness and reaction time may be seriously and adversely affected.

4. Work diligently to maintain an effective and productive feeder program. While greater attention will be paid to this vital area of coaching concern in Chapter 4, perhaps we should note at this point that, *Where winning traditions are concerned, building and/or maintaining an effective feeder program is the single most important step a coach can take concerning successful program continuity.* The more skilled athletes a coach has to work with, the more likely he is to win consistently—and below the college level, at least, the feeder program is the coach's best means for ensuring a steady supply of young athletes to replace those lost to graduation.

5.   Don't let the team grow complacent about winning.   You don't have to teach winners how to win, but you have to keep them hungry. It is always a mistake to assume that, just because a winning tradition has developed over a number of years, the players no longer need to be challenged or motivated. If lack of a productive feeder program represents the successful program's first step downhill toward mediocrity, the second step occurs when a sense of complacency, or lack of challenge, sets in. When this happens, it is because the coach has not worked hard enough in terms of finding new ways to stimulate and challenge his players toward higher levels of excellence.

Players should not be expected to motivate themselves, set their own goals, or assess the effectiveness of their efforts to achieve those goals. The coach who hopes to continue to win consistently will strive constantly to stay ahead of the players in every respect, including knowledge of the game, enthusiasm and devotion to the team, and ability to set, evaluate, and redefine goals in such a manner as to keep the players working hard to improve the quality of their performances, both individually and as a team.

6.   Keep a low-key public profile where winning is concerned.   Even if you privately expect to win every game for at least the next decade or so, you should avoid the temptation to share those expectations publicly with anyone, especially the news media.

In 1969, Joe Namath brashly predicted that his New

York Jets football team would upset the highly favored Baltimore Colts in Super Bowl III. He astonished the sports world by leading his Jets to a 16–7 victory—but most coaches agree that the road to success does not normally involve exhibiting a superior public attitude, or goading or belittling opponents.

What it boils down to is this: the fewer promises you make, the less you have to apologize for if you fall short. It is far better for you to promise little and deliver more than you predicted than to receive blame for the grandiose promises that you couldn't keep.

The fool boasts about his victories *before* the game is played. The unthinking person brags *after* his wins are achieved. The wise man *never* boasts about his wins, but gives endless credit to all concerned (including the opponent) for a game well played.

It all goes back to a coaching principle that will be discussed in greater detail in Chapter 7; namely, that you should never give opponents a reason to want to defeat you; instead, you should make them find their own reasons for wanting to win. If, whether by comments made to the news media by you or your players or by other means, you manage to incite the opponents, you can be sure of at least one thing: you've made the opposing coach's job easier than it would have been otherwise, by motivating his players for him. And you can bet that he isn't going to return the favor by motivating your players for you.

DEFINE YOUR TEAM AS A WINNING TEAM

In this chapter we have considered winning and losing as situations that arise not primarily because of luck, divine providence, or chance, but as the result of previous experiences that tend to define us in our own minds (or in others' minds) as either winners or losers. Our experiences give us the confidence to face new challenges, or else they shackle us to the bonds of our past failures, depending upon the quality of those experiences.

We learn to win, we learn to lose. As coaches we try to teach other people—our players—how to win, or at least how to keep from losing. Yet does it not stand to reason that our success in this endeavor will depend to a very great extent upon our own personal understanding of the elements most commonly associated with winning, together with the depth of our commitment to the pursuit and achievement of those factors?

In Chapter 2 we study the ways that coaches approach the task of winning, and we find, not surprisingly, that the success they encounter in the long run is directly related to the depth and scope of their dedication, commitment, and work habits.

THE DRIVE
TO WIN—
A CONTINUUM
OF EXPECTATIONS

chapter **2**

As a man thinketh, so is he.

—Proverbs 23:7

Winning isn't everything, but wanting to win is.

—Vince Lombardi

Winning isn't everything, but it beats anything that comes in second.

—Bear Bryant

Somewhere in this chapter you're likely to come face to face with every coach that you've ever played for, or known, or read about, or coached against—identified not by name, of course, but rather by the personality characteristics and relative drive to win that they bring to their coaching. You're in here too, and so am I. And if we are honest with ourselves about where we are to be found within this continuum of coaching expectations, it shouldn't be too hard for us to understand why we win or lose as often as we do.

Eleven categories of coaches have been identified, ranging from those at one end of the continuum who expect to lose to those at the other end of the spectrum who will stop at nothing (including cheating or condoning dirty play) in order to win. Of course, the possibility exists that a subcategory or two might have been overlooked somewhere along the way, but the vast majority of coaches are represented in the pages that follow.

1.   COACHES WHO EXPECT TO LOSE

In his best-selling book *Games People Play*,* the late psychiatrist and author Eric Berne wrote that some people choose mates who they know will never be able to make them happy. They do so, Dr. Berne contended, because they are basically unhappy themselves, and marrying someone who cannot possibly make them happy gives them someone

---

*New York: Grove Press, 1964.

to blame for their unhappiness. He also speculated that, being basically unhappy people, they are "happier" in their familiar role of complaining about their miserable marriages than they would be in a really good marriage that gave them nothing to complain about. They are, in short, "happier being unhappy," if that makes any sense. They feel guilty about whatever successes come their way, and only in failure are they truly comfortable.

If you've ever known a married couple who "can't live with each other, and can't live without each other," this is the kind of situation Dr. Berne was writing about.

Bear in mind that we aren't talking about people making conscious decisions to foul up their lives; it isn't a matter of a man's deciding that "I believe I'll marry her because she'll make me unhappy," any more than a person enters coaching for the express purpose of losing as many games as possible. The culprit here is the subconscious mind, the true face beneath the public mask we wear.

A casual acquaintance who loves nothing better than a good poker game once told me that at any table of seven players, you'll always find one or two consistent winners, three or four players who win sometimes and lose sometimes, and one or two players who lose heavily every single time they sit down to play. It is the latter category that most interests me: Don't they know that they're terrible poker players? Don't they realize that they're just throwing away their money?

No, my friend replied when I asked him those questions, *they honestly believe that, no matter how much or how often they've lost in the past, tonight will be the night when they turn it all around. And when the game is over and they've lost again, they're already thinking that next time will be their long-awaited payoff. But they never do anything to improve their play. They just keep losing and losing.**

---

*"In gambling, the deadly sin is to mistake bad play for bad luck."—Ian Fleming.

There's good news and bad news here. The bad news is that, if you're this type of person and coach, you'll probably never know it, not even if (or when) your losses finally cost you your job or force you out of coaching altogether.

The good news is, in fact, twofold: first, there probably aren't many coaches who fall into this category; and second, if you aren't this type of coach, you'll win close to 100 percent of your games played against coaches who are in this category.

2. COACHES WHO DON'T CARE ABOUT WINNING

A perfect example of this type of coach was given in Chapter 1: the coach who, after defeats, devotes no more than five or ten minutes at best to wondering why his team lost, and then proceeds with life as if the loss were no more than a distant memory, dimly remembered, if at all. (Note: we aren't saying that coaches should agonize endlessly over their defeats like a bad dream that won't go away—but if we don't study our losing performances to find ways to avoid repeating them, we probably *will* repeat them. As Benjamin Disraeli, a nineteenth-century British prime minister, pointed out, "Those who fail to learn from the mistakes of history are condemned to repeat them.")

Category 2 coaches may appear to be capable technicians in their jobs; they may even have good teams from time to time. But on the other hand, they tend to treat their coaching as a pastime or leisure-time activity, not as a full-time job. And because they do not possess an overriding desire to win, they cannot transmit such desire to their players.

Oh, they put in the official hours on the job, all right—teaching their classes during the school day, practicing in the afternoon or even scouting opponents from time to time. But something's missing, and that something is the attention to detail that separates the good coaches from the pretenders. The coach who doesn't really care about winning generally avoids the tedium of preparing detailed daily practice schedules, game plans, or scouting reports. (Regarding the latter, he is likely to treat scouting trips as a chance to socialize with other coaching acquaintances who are scouting the same game.)

Too, at practice he may not want to spend any great amount of time working on the basic individual fundamental skills which are so important to the development of young and inexperienced players, preferring instead to devote most (or *all*, in some cases) of his practice time to scrimmaging or team patterns. He is not terribly interested in learning more about his sport than he already knows; as a result, he tends to use the same offenses and defenses year after year because he understands them, and not because they are best for his team. Thus, he is rather predictable in his coaching, which makes it easy for opponents to prepare for him except when he is blessed with exceptionally talented players.

3. COACHES TO WHOM WINNING IS OF SECONDARY IMPORTANCE

This category is so closely related to the previous one as to be almost the same thing—almost, but not quite. While winning is important to Category 3 coaches, other goals are equally or more important to them. Their parallel may be seen in parents who want the team to win, but not if it means that their son or daughter will warm the bench most of the time.

What sort of goals are we talking about? Well, for starters, I once knew a coach whose primary goal was to have his players like him. (Presumably he felt that, since he was fresh out of college and hadn't been in coaching long enough to have earned his players' respect, he could accomplish that goal by gaining their friendship.) Thus, he allowed his players to chew tobacco at basketball practice, and he even double-dated with his high school players from time to time. (He attempted to justify his double dates by pointing out that he wasn't really double-dating; he was merely chaperoning his players on dates. "Besides," he confided, "it isn't like *my* date is a high school student at my school." Indeed, she wasn't: she was a 17-year-old student at another high school in the area.)

Ivan Duncan, who was an assistant basketball coach for Coach Jerry Tarkanian at the University of Nevada at Las Vegas in the early 1970s, once remarked, "Show me a basketball coach who plays golf in his spare time, and I'll show you a loser." And while his statement is rather extreme, it points to the kind of conflict of interest that we're discussing here.

Consider the following hypothetical situation: Coach A and Coach B are both coaching baseball teams who lately have been taking their lumps. Coach A, an avid tennis player, tries to get in a set or two of tennis every afternoon after baseball practice, except on game days or days when his bowling team is scheduled to perform that night. His weekends are pretty much tied up with those activities, too.

Coach B, on the other hand, also loves to participate in those sports—but presently he finds little enjoyment in tennis or golf because his baseball team is not performing well and he suspects that he is not doing all that he might to improve his team's chances of winning. As a result, he spends much of his spare time during afternoons, evenings, and weekends searching for ways to reverse his team's fortunes.

Now you tell me: which of those two coaches is more likely to solve his baseball team's problems, Coach A or Coach B?

4. LAZY COACHES

This type of coach is familiar enough in coaching or in any other line of work. He is basically a lazy person. He wants to win all right, but he expects others to do his work for him. In coaching, he expects his assistant coaches and/or players to work harder than he does to achieve team goals. He may or may not take credit for wins, but more often than not he privately blames his assistants or players for the team's losses.

Most important, he is not aware that he is not a hard worker. He doesn't realize that he could be working much harder, or that by his lazy work habits he is short-changing his team and creating an unfair double standard of performance. He probably believes (because he *wants* to believe it) that he is working just as hard as any of his coaching peers, even those who are achieving far greater successes with their teams than *he* is with *his* teams.

Moreover, he sees little correlation between the amount of time and effort spent in his coaching and the level of success achieved in his coaching. He doesn't understand workaholics, and he believes that he can accomplish as much as they can in far less time and with considerably less effort.

He does not understand that, in coaching as in life, *the pursuit of excellence or victory is a full-time job.*

What *does* he understand, then?

The Category 4 coach understands that, if he only had better players, he would achieve better results. As one college football coach who shall remain nameless said, "I give the same half-time speech over and over. It works best when my players are better than the other coach's players."

Well, sure it does, Coach! But have you ever considered the possibility of giving a *different* half-time speech? (And who recruited those duds that you give the same, useless half-time speech to, anyway?)

5. COMPLACENT COACHES

Even if you're not a particularly religious person, you may find great inspiration in the famous prayer of Protestant theologian Reinhold Niebuhr:

God grant me the courage to change those things which can be changed; the serenity to accept those things which cannot be changed; and the wisdom to know the difference.

(Undoubtedly, the Category 4 coach would add to this prayer, . . . *and give me someone like Isiah Thomas to be "a coach on the floor" for me.)*

The Category 5 coach wouldn't add anything at all to the Reverend Niebuhr's beautiful prayer; in fact, he likely would subtract the first and last points, after which it would read, "Grant me the serenity to accept whatever comes my way."

Such coaches tend to have a bland, passive approach to their coaching. They don't often take chances, because "gambles can backfire and beat you." They are seldom fiery, emotional coaches because "that kind of stuff can kill you or give you ulcers." They tend to accept whatever Fate is kind and cruel enough to bring them, whether it be championship teams or clunkers.

Other characteristics of Category 5 coaches include the following. First, they tend to adopt certain styles of play and stay with them throughout their careers rather than experimenting with new or different systems, and while there's nothing wrong *per se* with using such an approach, the reasoning behind their refusing to change is questionable. Because they have accepted their lot for better or worse, they are unlikely to make any kind of drastic changes in their philosophy or system of play, *not even when the need for such change is clearly indicated, and when such changes would be in the team's best interests.*

Second, such coaches are likely to harbor secret jealousies concerning other coaches who have better material to work with. In this respect, Category 4 and 5 coaches are alike: when things aren't going well for them, they both tend to wish that they had someone else's superior players. While wishful thinking doesn't hurt anyone, it is nonproductive in the sense that, like daydreaming, it doesn't get anything done. It doesn't solve problems, and it wastes time that could be better spent searching for solutions to one's problems.

6.   INEXPERIENCED COACHES

Actually, this pivotal category in the middle of our list of coaching characteristics is composed of two subheadings; namely, coaches who lack playing and/or coaching experience in their sport, and coaches who have never bothered to study their sport. Let's look at each type.

Coaches who lack playing and/or coaching experience in a given sport.   Particularly among young coaches who are just starting out in the profession with little more than their own high school experience as a guide to prepare them for their initial coaching experience, it is only natural that they should rely heavily on the drills, plays, and systems that their own high school coaches used. As they mature as coaches, however, their coaching skills broaden considerably, and they tend to adopt or develop styles of play that reflect their own newly emerging philosophies rather than mirroring those of their previous coaches.

At least that's the way the good young coaches learn the ropes in their profession. As for the rest, well, because they see no need to *study*, they are unlikely to progress beyond the limits of their previous experience and present level of coaching skills. That's why this category is pivotal and crucial: every year, young, inexperienced coaches enter the profession, fresh out of college and eager to take on the challenge of coaching. In a sense, they're like baby birds leaving the nest for the first time, innocently and blissfully unaware of the awesome challenges and responsibilities facing them. One can't help but wonder, too, how many of them will be able to survive the ordeal without being chewed up and spit out by the system. As you already know if you've been around coaching for awhile, it's a difficult, demanding occupation even if done badly, and in order to survive and *succeed*, the young coach's first decisions absolutely *must not* be made on the basis of expediency!

These decisions—how receptive they will be to new concepts and techniques (new for *them*, at any rate); how flexible and adaptable they will be in their thinking; and how hard they will work to fill in the gaps in their knowledge—will either limit them to mediocrity, if they are initially close-minded, or open them to a universe of potential for success in coaching, if they are constantly searching for ways to expand their present level of awareness and understanding.

This is hardly an exaggeration. In order to achieve any kind of lasting success in coaching, one must be flexible and adaptable to change, or else the times will pass him by. In all team sports, the emphasis shifts between offense and defense, and within these areas new and exciting styles of play are constantly emerging. The coach who does nothing to keep in step with these changes is likely to find himself steamrollered by progress.

Consider, for example, the advent of the triple-option offense in football. Although it appears that defenses at last may have caught up with the triple option's three-pronged attack, such was not the case during the 1970s, when college football powers such as Oklahoma, Southern Cal, Nebraska, Texas, Houston, and Alabama used powerful wishbone, I-formation, and veer running attacks to routinely demolish opponents by 30-to-40-point margins. The triple option was at one time thought to be unstoppable by many coaches, but how many still agree that triple-option attacks cannot be defensed?

Today the emphasis on offense has in some cases shifted toward wide-open passing attacks, with rifle-armed quarterbacks passing as often as 50 to 60 times a game. And you can bet that even now, defensive coaches all over the nation are burning the midnight oil searching for ways to effectively combat this new trend.

If you are a young coach who is just starting out in coaching, the two best tools you can bring with you are an open mind—the desire to improve yourself as well as your players—and a willingness to work as hard as necessary to overcome all obstacles to your success.

Coaches who have never bothered to study their sport.   Being young and inexperienced is not the only reason some coaches don't know enough about their sport to teach their players the fundamental skills. There are also coaches who, for any number of reasons (such as close-mindedness, laziness, or having good athletes initially and seeing no further reason to expand their knowledge), have never made the decision to master their sport. Instead, they have limited themselves largely to what they already knew about their sport when they entered coaching. If they've managed to survive somehow despite their deficiencies, they may have picked up bits and pieces of coaching philosophy, tactics, teaching techniques, and drills here and there, but their overall grasp of the game is generally little more advanced than that of their players.

And if you doubt that such coaches exist, consider the following.

The luckiest coach I ever knew was a junior college basketball coach during the mid-1960s. After winning two state high school championships, he was named head basketball coach at a junior college that had a winning tradition in basketball. He was quite successful there too, winning 20 or more games at least twice and 19 games the year I was at school—and the guy couldn't coach a lick! (But that was all right, because he was an even worse recruiter.)

Once, in a close game in which his team was behind by one point with time running out, he called a timeout while his team had the ball. I moved closer to the bench in order to hear what he said to his players. When they were seated and ready for his last-second strategy, he glanced up at the clock with a worried expression on his face, rubbed his hands nervously, checked the clock again, and then leaned forward.

"Fellas," he said in a choked voice, "we gotta win this game!" Then he turned and walked away to get a drink of water, leaving it to his assistant coach to add anything meaningful, such as how they might go about setting up their last-second shot. And wouldn't you believe it, his point guard hit a 30-footer at the buzzer to win the game!

Now, I try not to be too critical of other coaches, having been there before myself, but really: how could anyone even survive in coaching, let alone establish this coach's impressive credentials, without learning something about the sport he was coaching somewhere along the way? As I said, he was lucky.

In his first high school coaching job, he inherited a powerhouse girls' basketball team that breezed to a state title. And when he took another job coaching boys' basketball, one of his seniors that year was named most valuable player at the state high school all-star game and later earned all-SEC honors three years in a row. Another senior on that same team later became a starting forward at a well-known NCAA Division I school. That was state championship number two.

Then, when he got the junior college head coaching job, his assistant coach was a marvelously gifted ex-SEC star whose basketball knowledge was boundless, exceeded only by his recruiting skills. (The year I was at the school, they recruited seven players: the head coach recruited one player, sight unseen, who was 5'10" and played a total of three minutes that season, while the assistant coach signed six quality athletes who stood 6'5", 6'7", 6'8", 6'8", 6'10" and 6'11" respectively.)

The moral of the story is that some people manage to beat the odds without meaning to, but if you begin your coaching career expecting luck rather than hard work to be your greatest ally, you're apt to be sadly mistaken. As the late, great Yankee baseball slugger Roger Maris said, "You win not by chance, but by preparation."

7. COACHES WHO LET THEIR EXPECTATIONS RULE THEIR EMOTIONS

Coaching is a difficult job, characterized in equal part by the exhilarating thrill of hard-earned victories* and the soul-crushing heartache of bitter defeats.† The pressure to

---

*"When you win, nothing hurts."—Joe Namath

†"No one knows what to say in the loser's locker room."—Muhammad Ali

win, whether externally or self-imposed, can be enormous. As a result, many coaches find themselves in a constant struggle to balance the emotional highs and lows in their lives. Balance is important because, while the emotional highs are a welcome reward for a job well done, the lows can—if left unchecked—wreck one's physical and mental health, create family problems, and drive even the best of coaches out of the profession.

The coach we're describing here—the Category 7 coach—is one who initially has high expectations for success and winning (which may or may not be realistic), but then, when Fate deals him a few unexpected setbacks and things begin to fall apart, he gives up on his team and merely goes through the motions of coaching for the rest of the season because *this* team cannot meet his expectations. Because he cannot attain the highs that he seeks, he elects to soften the effect of the lows by reducing his expectations to that of the Category 5 coach, who calmly accepts his lot for better or worse.

The problem could have been avoided if he hadn't set such store in his expectations in the first place. Surely he was aware of Murphy's Law; why, then, does he expect incredible successes, rather than merely working to the best of his ability to achieve them and accepting them whenever they occur? The answer is, of course, that this coach is an incurable optimist, which is all right if you're a level-headed, even-dispositioned sort of person, but can be devastating if you're highly emotional.

This is not to imply that optimists are misguided in their thinking; after all, every coach expects to win his share and more of the games he coaches, whether by virtue of his coaching ability, his players' skills, or possibly divine intervention. Still, it is sometimes difficult to understand the thinking of the eternal optimist who sees silver linings in every funnel cloud.

At any rate, Category 7 coaches are an endangered species, at least until such time as they learn to control the extent to which they let their expectations rule their emotions.

If the pressure of their expectations of winning becomes too great, they are likely to quit coaching—which is a shame too, because many of them are potentially top-notch coaches.

8. OVERLY CONSERVATIVE COACHES

Basically, there are three ways to win a game: (a) you can aggressively attack your opponents and win the game yourself; (b) you can avoid taking chances and wait for your opponents to beat themselves; or (c) if you and your players are good enough, you can blend those two styles of play to either defeat your opponents or let them beat themselves, as the situation dictates.

Our present concern is with certain coaches within style (b), which is used by far more coaches than (a) and (c) combined.

Most coaches are basically conservative; that is, they prefer to be in control of games at all times.* And since the surest method for maintaining control lies in not taking chances, most coaches tend to shy away from exotic, high-risk styles of play.† For example, when ex-head football Coach Darrell Royal of the University of Texas said, "Only three things can happen when you put the ball in the air—and two of them are *bad*," you just *knew* that the Longhorns weren't going to come out throwing the ball.

As with so many things in coaching and in life, though,

---

*"Before you win it, you have to not lose it."—Chuck Noll

†The recent trend toward complex, wide-open passing attacks in college football may not be as radical a departure from conservative running games as it appears; after all, if you're lucky enough to have a Herschel Walker in your backfield, necessity dictates that you run him as often as possible. Similarly, if you're lucky enough to have a uniquely talented individual such as Vinnie Testaverde quarterbacking your team, you don't want to waste his incredible passing skills and leadership ability by having him hand the ball off four out of every five plays.

Besides, the trend toward full-scale passing attacks has not filtered down to the high school ranks to any great extent, simply because most high school coaches aren't blessed with quarterbacks who can throw the ball or lead a team like Vinnie Testaverde.

there's good news and bad news here. The good news is that many of the best and most successful coaches in history have been basically conservative by nature—for example, basketball's Adolph Rupp, Joe B. Hall, Bobby Knight, Frank McGuire, and John Wooden, and football's Vince Lombardi, Bobby Dodd, Woody Hayes, George Halas, Bo Schembechler, and Vince Dooley. Being conservative-minded will not adversely affect your chances for success in coaching—except if you go overboard in trying not to lose games.

To paraphrase humorist James Thurber, *if you bend over backward too far in order to avoid losing games, you'll fall on your face.*

And *that's* the bad news: as the level of competition rises—say, in post-season playoffs or tournament games—the less likely a strictly conservative style of play will be to win the *big* games against opponents of equal or superior ability. (This is particularly true if they are better at their conservative style than our team is with ours.) There simply comes a time when every coach, regardless of how conservative his philosophy, must bend a little and take chances in order to win. (Unfortunately, some coaches will interpret this statement to mean passing on fourth-down-and-30 when they're behind by six in the fourth quarter with 0:30 showing on the clock, but that's not what I mean.)

A high school football coach had outstanding success for several years with his teams on the subregional and regional levels, using mainly basic Oklahoma defense and a relentless ground attack featuring a splendid bread-and-butter trap play. Only once in his ten years or more at the same school did he win less than seven games in a season, and that year his inexperienced squad won five games, due largely to his coaching ability.

On state level, though, his teams never seemed to rise to the occasion. They seldom, if ever, were blown out of games—his program development and conservative, power-oriented playing style saw to that—but they were never able to break through to the highest levels of state competition, to the everlasting disappointment of the team's fans and supporters.

Once limited to a conservative, ball-control style of play, it is very difficult to switch on relatively short notice to a more wide-open style of play. There is, of course, the old coaching adage that "you don't change horses in midstream." Our players, accustomed to a style of play that they already know and understand, may be understandably reluctant to switch to a radically different style on short notice, especially since it was the more conservative style that got them where they are. Anyway, most coaches probably wouldn't be comfortable with changes that go against the grain of their basic philosophy.

A coach should not be afraid to take chances. Fear of losing is one thing: it's an entirely different matter when a coach limits his potential for winning because he fears losing too greatly to take chances. Admittedly, sometimes those risks may fail, causing us to lose a game that we might otherwise have won. But on the other hand, without taking an occasional risk, we might never reach the point where a failed risk could win the big game.

This is not to say, of course, that a coach should not be conservative; still, when Team A—a power-oriented team—is playing Team B, and Team B is better at *its* power game than Team A is, Team B will win at least nine times out of ten in a purely strength-against-strength matchup. To ignore this fact, or to blithely proceed as if it were not so, is to fly in the face of reality. It is a dangerous and costly form of self-deception. The reality of the situation is, *when you decide to slug it out with a slugger, you'd better be pretty darned sure that your knockout punch is better than his*—or else you'd better have a couple of surprises up your sleeve like the "rope-a-dope" tactic that Muhammad Ali used to regain the world heavyweight boxing title from George Foreman in Zaire in 1974.

9. OVERLY AGGRESSIVE COACHES

These coaches are the antithesis of Category 8 coaches; that is, they will not hesitate to take aggressive risks in their coaching. Rather than waiting passively for victories to come to them via opponents' mistakes, Category 9 coaches prefer to use attacking offenses and defenses to create mistakes and control the tempo and outcomes of games. They are not always successful in this approach, of course, but they are always extremely difficult to coach against, even if their team play sometimes tends to be erratic. Their players tend to play with reckless abandon, mirroring the coach's gambler attitude, since their job is to make things happen rather than merely waiting for things to happen. They make mistakes, of course, and occasionally those mistakes beat them. But what so many coaches fail to understand is that, when rigorously applied, aggressive styles of play tend to force passive teams out of their style of play and tempo, and as a result those teams usually make more mistakes than they normally would, too.

Incidentally, there exists another subcategory of coach who, although basically conservative in his approach to his sport, will switch to aggressive styles of play when opportunities present themselves, or when he thinks that the change will benefit his team. Bear Bryant was such a coach; so was John Wooden in basketball, as are Dean Smith and John Thompson. They prefer to take what you give them—the conservative approach—but if you aren't giving them enough, they'll steal the rest by attacking your team like the Allies storming the beaches at Normandy on D-Day.

Such a diverse playing style has many advantages, not the least of which is that it's virtually impossible to adequately prepare your team for all the wrinkles that a Dean Smith-coached team is likely to throw at you. But be warned: if you want your basketball teams to play like the Tarheels, you'd better have a herd of thoroughbreds rather than plowhorses to work with: Coach Smith's system is incredibly complex, and requires smart, talented athletes to understand and take advantage of its complexities. (At a coaching clinic at which Charles G. "Lefty" Driesell and Smith were scheduled to speak, Lefty began his talk thus: "All of you intellectual coaches who came here to learn 47 different ways to play man-to-man defense the way Dean Smith does it at North Carolina can leave now. But all of you dumb blankety-blanks like me who would like to hear some simple stuff that you can understand and maybe use, stick around: you might learn something."

10. COACHES WITH A BURNING WILL TO WIN

Every coach prefers winning to losing, but not every coach feels the same burning compulsion to win. Not every coach is willing to make the sacrifices that sometimes are necessary to win. (Indeed, not every coach even realizes that such sacrifices are necessary.) And not every coach feels the same sense of pain in defeat that prompted Coach George Allen to say, "Every time you win, you're reborn; when you lose, you die a little."

It's not "only a game" to Category 10 coaches: it's an opportunity to affirm the values they hold dear. And because they approach the task of winning as if nothing else in life matters to them, they tend to be highly organized in their preparations for games.* They also tend to refuse to accept either the inevitability or finality of defeat: it had to be a Category 10 coach who first said "We weren't defeated; the clock just ran out before we could win." And because they approach the coaching task and winning with the single-mindedness of purpose of a killer whale homing in on its prey, they *do* win—most of the time.

11. COACHES WHO STOP AT NOTHING TO WIN

This type of coach is actually a Category 10 coach who cannot control his will to win. He will use whatever means at his disposal, whether fair or foul, and without the slight-

---

*Miami Dolphins' Head Coach Don Shula, describing George Allen, ex-head coach of the Washington Redskins: "He left nothing to chance, he prepared for everything. I remember he 'charted the sun' before our Super Bowl game in L.A. (in 1973)."

est sense of hesitation or remorse, in order to win. On occasion he may, either directly or indirectly, suggest to his players that they put a particular opposing player out of commission, or he may teach techniques that are questionable at best, and dangerously unethical at worst. (Two examples: first, a baseball coach teaches his players that, before taking their lead as base runners, they should first gather a handful of dirt to toss into the face of the player covering the base they intend to steal. Second, that same baseball coach teaches his players to slide with spikes held high in order to break up double plays in the most convincing manner possible.)

On the college level, the Category 11 coach "buys" high school prospects by offering them money, cars, or whatever else he thinks will induce them to sign a scholarship with his school.* If caught and confronted with his cheating, he falls back on the pale excuse that "everyone else is doing it, why shouldn't I?" But while big-time cheating is out of control in college athletics where recruiting is concerned, that fact does not excuse cheating.

Cheating is a shortcut to success in the same manner that bank robbery is a shortcut to wealth. Any coach who knowingly cheats or otherwise advocates unethical standards is a blight upon the reputation of the many thousands of honest, upright coaches in the profession.

When even one coach cheats, he makes all of us look bad.

---

*One particularly odious practice that has arisen and spread throughout the nation in recent years is that of athletic departments giving scholarships to attractive young coeds who agree to act as "hostesses" or "escorts" for the young male high school athletes who visit the campus as prospective signees.

A BURNING WITHIN: THE OVERACHIEVER'S APPROACH TO WINNING

Of course I want to win. I train for it. Fight for it. Suffer for it. And I'd kill any *man* for a win—but only during the event.

—*Hilda Svenson, ice skater*

If I was an owner, you know who I'd want riding my horse? Me. I want me because I want my jock, when he loses, to come back mad.

—*Bill Hartack, jockey*

There are coaches and there are coaches. All coaches want to win—but not, as we have seen, to the same extent. Some coaches are satisfied with winning occasionally; others agonize over every defeat like a death in the family.

All coaches work at their coaching, but some coaches go through the motions of coaching as if receiving their monthly paychecks were their primary goal and greatest reward in coaching. Other coaches approach their work with the single-mindedness of a great white shark on the prowl at mealtime.

In every profession there are certain individuals who, by virtue of their unique personalities and tireless work habits, are destined for success in their chosen field. No matter what obstacles are placed in their paths, they are able to endure, overcome adversity, and rise to the pinnacles of success in their profession. They are the overachievers who believe in the American dream that the greatest successes come to those who work hardest to achieve them. They believe, as did Helen Keller (who, although deaf and blind from birth, achieved world-wide fame as a best-selling author) that "We can do anything we want to if we stick to it long enough."

In this chapter, we shall explore the motivations, work habits, rewards, and frustrations of the overachievers in the coaching profession—the Category 10 coaches who possess a burning desire to win and win and win. In so doing, we are likely to find that, by adjusting our goals, expectations, and work habits, we can achieve successes that previously would have been possible only in our wildest flights of imagination.

HOW TO WIN BY TAKING ADVANTAGE OF NATURAL FLAWS

A perfect diamond is nature's most perfect gemstone. Still, the most famous diamond in the world—the Hope diamond, which is on permanent display at the Smithsonian Institution in Washington, D.C.—is imperfect, flawed. It is this flaw that gives the Hope diamond its deep, lustrous blue color. An otherwise-perfect sapphire, ruby, or emerald is similarly flawed, for without such flaws, each would be colorless. In each case, their flaws, however slight, lend beauty and lasting value to the gemstones.

So it is with coaching. Even the very best of coaches is flawed. Everyone makes mistakes, although hopefully we learn from our mistakes most of the time. (Or, as Dr. Laurence Peter, author of *The Peter Principle*, has pointed out, if we aren't going to learn from our mistakes, we're better off not making them.)

We are flawed, all of us—but the best among us are able to find ways to use those flaws constructively to achieve great things, rather than giving in to their weaknesses and admitting that they cannot be the kind of person they want to be or achieve what they want in life.

Using the Fear of Failure as a Motivating Force

In itself, fear is basically an unhealthy, negative emotion. It is only when we begin to conquer our fears that anything positive arises out of fear. Yet fear is necessary, both to the athlete and the coach. We should not want to lose our fears, but rather to control them. When we lose our fears entirely, we become complacent and lazy.

As William Shakespeare wrote in *Measure for Measure*,

Our doubts are traitors
And make us lose the good we oft might win,
By fearing to attempt.

As a motivating force in athletics, the greatest fear is *fear of failure*. And because success and failure in sports normally are associated, whether rightly or wrongly, with winning and losing, it follows that many coaches and athletes are driven to win often and consistently because they do not want to lose.* To them, defeats are more than mere losses; they are public evidence of personal failure. And since the only way to erase the stigma of personal failure is to win every game, that is precisely the goal of Category 10 coaches, who are impelled by their fear of failure. Nothing less than winning every game satisfies their need to escape a sense of personal failure. They will do anything and everything in their power to avoid losing, simply because losing is, in their estimation, for losers.

Pursuing Lofty Expectations

As golfing great Jack Nicklaus put it, "In golf, you're always breaking a barrier. When you bust it, you set yourself a little higher barrier, and try to break that one."

In his excellent book *Pro*, the diary of a year on the professional golf tour, Frank Beard described Nicklaus and Arnold Palmer as possessing an incredible, burning intensity to win every event on the tour. *They don't just want to win*, he wrote, *they have to win. And they'll do practically anything that is legally and morally acceptable in order to win.* And having won, we might add, they were able to quickly shrug off the victory in order to prepare themselves mentally and physically for the next event on the tour. (Nicklaus in particular was known to return to the driving

---

*"Why did I want to win? Because I didn't want to lose."—Max Schmeling, ex-heavyweight boxing champion

range or putting green for further practice immediately after receiving his paycheck in victories in which he was dissatisfied with a particular aspect of his play.)

While the potential for frustration is great when we are pursuing lofty goals, the potential for lofty achievement is equally great. Regardless of whose expectations or approval we are striving toward—a parent's, a coach's, or our own—if the expectations mean everything to us, we will consistently give our all to meet those expectations. We won't be satisfied with a half-hearted effort unless we're also satisfied with others' disapproval or our own.*

Achieving a Sense of Self-Accomplishment

This includes pride in individual accomplishment; self-fulfillment; ego enhancement, or creating a positive self-image; mastery or control of others (that is, opponents); and functioning as a contributing member of a team that is committed to the pursuit of worthwhile goals. Any or all of these reasons can provide the incentive for the pursuit of greatness rather than mediocrity.

Desiring Revenge

Although not normally considered to be a powerful long-term motivator, the desire for revenge sometimes can burn deeply enough within an individual to impel him or her in worthwhile directions. In my own case, for example, I first became seriously interested in basketball as a sixth grader when my classmates on the school's Gra-Y basketball team wouldn't let me play in a game that was a blowout in our favor. (We had no coach; the "coaching" was done by the two best players on our team.) I cried all the way home from the Savannah YMCA that day, and I vowed that some-

---

*"We can secure other people's approval, if we do right and try hard; but our own is worth a hundred of it, and no way has been found out of securing that."—Mark Twain

day I'd be a good enough basketball player to make them pay for not letting me play.

Admittedly, it was a childish response on my part, but after all, I was eleven years old at the time. And from that day on, basketball was an important part of my life. I can recall shooting by myself in my backyard, hour after hour, practically every day for nearly two years, before I dared to play anyone. I devised shooting games to pass the time, and in my mind it was always me playing one or the other of the boys who wouldn't let me in the game that day.*

Pursuing a Goal with Single-Mindedness of Purpose

I've always believed that, as good a football coach as he was, the late Paul "Bear" Bryant would have been just as great at coaching swimming, gymnastics, tennis, baseball, or tiddledy winks. He hinted as much himself when he said, "I ain't nothin' but a *winner*." Alabama's Bear wasn't bragging; he was merely stating a fact.

Let's face it: the man knew how to *win*. He knew what he wanted, and he knew how to get it. He understood people, and he knew how to get the best out of his players. To his dying day, he was a student of the game of football, and he would have brought those same positive qualities to *any* sport he coached. If, say, *lacrosse* had been his chosen sport, he'd have attacked it with the same enthusiasm and relentless zeal—and love—that he brought to his football coaching. He would not accept less than excellence and victory, whether from himself, his assistant coaches, his players, or anyone else even remotely connected with his program.

Incidentally, Bear's early motivation toward excellence and winning grew out of his fear of having to return to his hometown of Moro Bottom, Arkansas, as a failure. This de-

---

*Seven years after the incident at the YMCA, I happened to face one of the two boys in a church league basketball game. I outscored him, 33–0. And although the desire for revenge was long since past as a motivator for my basketball performances, that game remains one of my sweetest memories as a player.

sire to escape a life of poverty (as in Bear's case), or an unhappy home life, or whatever one considers to have been a
previously unsatisfactory existence, is commonly encountered in many walks of life. In sports, it can provide a powerful and lasting motivation toward winning, among players
as well as coaches.

THE MINUSES OF A BURNING DESIRE TO WIN

As is true of virtually everything associated with human existence, there are advantages and disadvantages to
the sort of coaching with which this chapter is concerned.

Among the disadvantages of such an approach to
coaching, probably the most serious negative factor is that
the unbridled desire to win every game may lead the overzealous coach to the temptation to cheat, to abuse players in
the name of winning, or to use other questionable or unethical coaching practices such as instructing players to deliber-
ately injure opponents. Of course, it doesn't have to be that
way; still, the opportunity always exists when winning is
afforded equal or greater importance than the joy of playing
the game.

A second disadvantage is that, if one dedicates his entire life to the pursuit of victory and excellence, he may find
later in life that he has missed out on such simple and irre-
trievable pleasures as spending time with his family and
watching his children grow up. And while in many cases
that's the price one has to pay for achieving excellence in
his chosen profession, it can prove to be a costly decision to
live with.

A third disadvantage concerning coaching intensity is
that some coaches cannot control their intensity; instead,
they let it control them and their actions, to the eventual
detriment of all concerned. Such coaches tend to be excellent on a short-term basis because—initially, at least—their
players like their intense approach to the game. Their passion for the sport is admirable, but rightly or wrongly, they

tend to expect a similar degree of passionate devotion from each and every player. And there's the rub: the fiery coach who cannot understand or accept the fact that a given player (or players) on his team are not highly motivated the way he is on a 24-hour basis, may soon find that those players are turned off by his whirlwind, faster-than-sound and louder-than-a-747-jetliner approach to coaching. He may lose the ability to communicate with them because he has no respect for "lazy slackers who are more interested in their stock portfolios or love lives than in performing repetitive fundamental drills." The players, in turn, are likely to be repelled by the childishness (or insanity) of a grown man who uses his "love for the game" as an excuse to browbeat and intimidate people that he doesn't like.

Such coaches generally do not last long in coaching—or, at least, they seldom remain for long in any given coaching situation. Their insatiable intensity tends to repulse players, fans, boosters, and academic colleagues alike—on a long-range basis, at least. In order for such coaches to remain at one school for a long period of time (and it *has* been done before), three factors must occur or be present: (1) the coach must win immediately; (2) he must win consistently; and most important of all, (3) he must be coaching in a situation where the fans and boosters accept his behavior as eccentric rather than detrimental to the emotional development and well-being of his players.

In short, he must be coaching in a situation where the fans and boosters want to win as much as *he* does.

THE PLUSES OF A BURNING DESIRE TO WIN

On the other hand, there is the inescapable fact that the overachiever's approach to coaching *works*. It brings home the wins over the long haul. If you study the work habits of any coach in any sport who wins more often than the majority of his peers, you will find that he is at heart a Category 10 coach. He does more things well than most of his peers because he works harder than they do to achieve what he wants. He wins not by accident, but by virtue of a deep and abiding commitment to what he believes in.

Another positive advantage of such a thorough and dedicated approach to coaching is that it gives concrete meaning and direction to one's work to a greater extent than other, less urgent approaches. Coach George Allen has stated his belief that we are put here on earth to accomplish tasks, and the quality of our lives is determined by the extent to which we pursue those tasks.

A third advantage is that, in setting and pursuing lofty goals, we have the opportunity to exert a positive, lasting influence upon players who may have never before been challenged to strive with every fiber of their being toward excellence. And as we attract an increasing number of players into our program who believe as we do, we are permitted to share with them the deep sense of community and commitment that grows out of the dedicated pursuit of excellence and winning.

Finally, there is the fact that the pursuit of greatness never yields a life of mediocrity. Great efforts always pay great dividends sooner or later. As Harry Truman once said, "I studied the lives of great men and famous women, and I found that the men and women who got to the top were those who did the job they had in hand, with everything they had of energy and enthusiasm and hard work."

THE COACH, PLAYERS, AND WINNING TEACHING METHODS

chapter **4**

I hear and I forget. I see and I remember. I do and I understand.

—*Chinese Proverb*

The mediocre teacher tells. The good teacher explains. The superior teacher demonstrates. The great teacher inspires.

—*William Arthur Ward*

NINE USEFUL CHARACTERISTICS OF COACHES

1. Determination and Resilience

Enough has already been said about this topic in Chapters 1 through 3 that it hardly needs mentioning at this point. As Abraham Lincoln once said,

> I do the very best I know how—the very best I can; and I mean to keep doing so until the end. If the end brings me out all right, what is said against me won't amount to anything. If the end brings me out wrong, ten angels swearing I was right would make no difference.

2. Patience

Building a winning program where none existed previously requires patience*; so do teaching skills, communicating ideas, dealing with personal problems, and virtually every other aspect of the coaching task. Admittedly, it's difficult to watch calmly as a youngster makes the same mistake 15 times in a row, especially when the skill is one that *we* could perform correctly in our sleep, handcuffed, blindfolded, and with our legs tied together. But the alternative—impatience—breeds frustration and a loss of confidence that is not easily regained. So we may as well strive

---

*"Let us run with patience the race that is set before us." —Hebrews 12:1

for patience in dealing with life's problems and our players' shortcomings. As Arnold Glasow put it, "You get the chicken by hatching the egg—not by smashing it."

3.   A Sense of Humor

Although we don't normally tend to think of coaches as being funny people, some of them have cultivated great senses of humor in their outlook toward coaching. College basketball's clown prince of humor, Abe Lemons, has suggested (among other things) that the way to end the collegiate recruiting wars for big men in basketball is to do away with the basket entirely and cut a circular hole in the floor to serve as the hoop. If you did that, Lemons said, there'd soon be a furious scramble among college coaches to recruit midgets and dwarfs.

Lemons also said that he'd "rather be a football coach (than a basketball coach). That way, you only lose 11 games a year."

Ex-USC head football coach John McKay once was asked why he let O. J. Simpson carry the ball so often—a stupid question if ever there was one. McKay's reply was, "It's not very heavy, you know."

Tampa Bay Buccaneer head coach Leeman Bennett was asked if it hurt him to see his young quarterback Steve Young running with the ball. Bennett replied, "Why should it hurt me? *He's* the one getting tackled."

Discussing his recruiting methods, Jerry Tarkanian explained, "I like to recruit junior college players; their cars are already bought and paid for." And when he signed his son Danny to a basketball scholarship at UNLV, Jerry confided, "The kid was easy to recruit; I bought him a car when he was 16, and I've been having an affair with his Mom for years."

Oklahoma University's Barry Switzer offered a common-sense reason why he was a natural edge in in-state recruiting over rival Oklahoma State University: "OU is easier to spell than OSU."

It's important to be able to see the funny side of situations, or at least to recognize that things could be worse. (I've always liked the closing line that comedian Steve Martin uses in his concert tour: "You've been a great audience, ladies and gentlemen. We've had a lot of fun here tonight, considering that sooner or later we're all gonna *die*.")

4. Generosity

Generosity includes willingness to at least share the credit for victory with players and assistant coaches, and to recognize and reward the efforts of all those who work to make our program operate smoothly and efficiently. (If you've ever considered coaching a thankless job, you should try working in the concession stand or ticket booth while the games are going on.)

5. Common Sense and Level-Headedness

Much, if not all, of coaching involves either solving problems or anticipating and avoiding them before they arise. Thus, coaches must take their work seriously enough to avoid wasting time whenever possible, which in turn means adopting a common-sense approach to problem solving.

6. A Mature Outlook and Demeanor

Although it's true that we coaches often wear casual clothing such as shorts and sneakers in our work, we are not children. Beyond all else, our players look to us for leadership and guidance, and we fail them in this regard if we attempt to relate to them as a friend first and as a coach second, or if we try to relate to them or gain their friendship on their level of maturity rather than our own.*

---

*This is not to say that we should not try to understand their problems from their point of view, but merely to suggest that, having listened to them, we should help them to find mature approaches to solving their problems.

I've known coaches who attended teenage parties for the purpose of drinking with their players. I've seen coaches get into fights with their players. I've seen coaches square off against their assistant coaches, and opposing coaches and players, and game officials, and fans too—but I've never seen anything good come of it.

7. A Businesslike Approach to Daily Practice and Game Preparation

For all intents and purposes, the coach who does not adequately prepare himself or his team for competition is nothing more than a glorified babysitter. Yet we've all known coaches who would no more sit down and prepare a daily practice schedule or game plan than they could sprout wings and fly.

In the long run, a coach tends to attract and keep players in his program who accept his philosophy and values. If the coach is lazy or tends to give up whenever the going gets tough, the players will adopt similar outlooks and playing habits. And if the coach adopts a disciplined, businesslike approach to his work habits and preparations for practice and games, the players will tend to be equally serious in their own preparations.

8. Self-Confidence and Leadership Ability

Let's begin with the obvious: great coaches are great leaders; good coaches are good leaders; and poor coaches are poor leaders.

Our players look to us for leadership and guidance— but what *is* leadership, anyway?

It is the ability to organize and direct the efforts of a group toward desired ends. Leadership is effective to the extent that it utilizes the available manpower efficiently and to the greatest extent possible.

Some people are superior leaders at least partly by virtue of their birth order; that is, eldest sons and daughters likely received early leadership experiences by being left in charge of their younger brothers and sisters when Mom and Dad were away. In such circumstances, a youngster learns to make quick, accurate, and authoritative decisions; as a result, he is likely to be highly effective in positions of authority such as coaching later in his adult life.

For those who are not eldest sons or daughters, leadership experiences generally begin at a later stage of life than for their older brothers and sisters, so they have considerable ground to make up. It can be done, of course, but not without diligent effort. Still, that's as it should be: if coaching were easy, everyone in the profession would be a great coach.

Regarding *self-confidence*, we must realize that if we hope to make others believe in us, we must first believe in ourselves. We must have an unshakable belief in what we can accomplish through hard work and perseverance. When we communicate that belief to our players, we are by inference communicating our belief in *their* ability to achieve great things, too, since it is they and not us who will play the games along the way.

9. Humility

In my book *Coaching and Motivation*, I stated my belief that every coach should undergo at least one (but preferably not more than one) losing season, whether to keep us humble and grateful for our victories or to remind us that winning consistently requires an incredible amount of concentrated effort. The best coaches already know this, of course.

Maintaining a sense of humility means remembering what it took to get us where we are. In the same sense that nature has provided us with a remarkable inability to recall the exact details and depth of physical pain that we've suffered in the past, human nature has given us the unwanted ability to forget how much work it took for us to overcome obstacles to our success. If or when this occurs, it is because we have lost our humility, and thus our willingness to pay the price of victory.

HOW TO RECOGNIZE
THE GREATEST COACH IN THE WORLD

The greatest coach in the world is the one:

- Who loves his sport and coaching so much that he can't wait for practice every day.*
- Whose teaching methods and enthusiasm are such that he inspires his players to practice on their own, and in their free time, the skills he teaches them at daily practices.
- Who genuinely cares about his players both personally and professionally—and lets them know it.
- Who creates such a closely knit team that his players love each other as a second family, and as a result they feel a genuine sense of responsibility to their teammates and him in their athletic performances.

THE IMPORTANCE OF A FEEDER PROGRAM

"No man is an island," the poet John Donne wrote, "No man can stand alone." So it is with us, as coaches attempting to build or maintain a winning program in our sport. Try as we might, we cannot succeed without the help of other people at other levels of play who ultimately supply us with the young athletes who form our teams. There simply are not enough of us to spread among teams at the various lower levels of play, nor are there enough hours in the day for us to teach a full class load, coach our varsity squad, and attend to the needs of other teams as well.

If we intend to build a winning program in high

---

*"Nothing is really work unless you would rather be doing something else."
—James M. Barrie, author

school—or at the junior high or middle school level, for that matter—we need to initiate, improve, supervise, and/or maintain the development of the feeder program that supplies us with athletes. Our continued success at our present level of coaching depends to a great extent on the number and quality of athletes that come to us from whatever feeder system exists in our community.

Typically, if we're a high school varsity head coach, our immediate feeder program is the B-team or junior varsity (jayvee) team at our school, which probably is coached either by us or our assistant coach(es). That squad is fed by one or more junior high or middle schools—which in turn is fed by one or more elementary schools. Community recreation teams and youth leagues may be an additional source of young athletes, and therefore must also be considered a part of our feeder program even if they are not under our direct authority or jurisdiction. If they supply us with athletes, whether now or later, they are our concern if not our responsibility. We should not hesitate to give them all the help and support we can provide, since the better they are able to do their jobs, the easier our own job will be when their players are old enough to play for us.

How to Start a Feeder Program

The following section includes four guidelines concerning installing, improving, or overseeing the effectivenss of, your feeder program—beginning with the assumption that no effective, organized feeder program presently exists in your community.

1. Create an interest in (and thus a perceived need for) a feeder program. Among the adult population, this might involve addressing the PTA, various men's and women's clubs and civic groups, your board of education or county commissioners, or whoever else might be able to exert positive influence toward the provision of funds for an organized recreation program in the community or an effective physical education program in the elementary schools.

Among the children, creating an interest might involve organizing a local competition similar to the highly success-ful "Punt, Pass, and Kick" football competition or the "Hot Shot" concept in basketball, to cite two examples. It could also include giving talks to student groups at assemblies; working with elementary school physical education teachers to provide Saturday morning intramural competi-tion for youngsters; organizing teams to play brief half-time games at your varsity home games (which would serve the dual purpose of getting more adults to see your own team in action); or assisting in the formation of special skills teams of youngsters to put on, say, ball-handling exhibitions at your varsity home games. In every case, you are both creat-ing (or broadening) interest in your sport, and you are help-ing to provide ample opportunities for youngsters to get in-volved in your sport if they so desire.

2. Work with the coaches involved in the feeder pro-gram to make their jobs easier and increase their under-standing of your sport. In some cases, for example, in the formation of youth recreation leagues, you may even have to help find coaches for teams or assist recreation personnel in finding high school-age students to work in the recreation program. Of course, it is equally likely that you will not have to involve yourself in these chores, but you should be willing to pitch in and help in any way possible, and to whatever extent is necessary.

You should also work to build bonds of friendship and mutual respect between yourself and the coaches who com-prise your feeder program. One way to do this is to periodi-cally host informal get-togethers such as cookouts or dinner at a local steak house, at which time you may want to dis-cuss your own philosophy and goals, offer advice concern-ing problems that the coaches may be having, talk about re-cent events and trends in your sport, or simply get to know the coaches better and thereby gain their friendship, trust, and respect.

In addition, you might want to offer coaching advice—tactfully, of course—or coaching resources such as handouts or books from your own sport library in an effort to upgrade the coaches' understanding of the sport. If, as many coaches do, you prepare mimeographed player handbooks, you may want to run off a few extra copies to distribute to the coaches in your feeder program (who, in turn, may want to use them as guides in preparing their own player handbooks). You may even want to organize a one-day, weekend seminar or coaching clinic every year for those coaches, which will give you ample opportunities to offer constructive teaching suggestions, show them new and challenging drills that they may not have been aware of, and explain to them the importance of what they are doing within the overall context of what you—and they—are trying to accomplish.

Finally, you should take advantage of every opportunity to encourage them and offer compliments, recognition, and praise for the job they are doing, both in private talks and in your public comments to the media, etc. You should invite them to your sports banquet as honored guests, and possibly reward them with plaques of appreciation or some other gesture of thanks for a job well done.

3. If at all possible, attempt to install your system at lower levels of play, or at least strive to see that ample attention is paid to the teaching of basic skills. One of the most successful high school coaches in history was Wright Bazemore, who, in nearly three decades as head football coach of the Valdosta, Georgia, Wildcats, averaged an astonishing ten wins a year—a national record. Coach Bazemore also won 14 state championships along the way and established a football program that is still going strong more than a decade after he retired from active coaching.*

---

*Coach Bazemore's career record included 290 wins and only 43 losses in 29 years of head coaching.

Among the many secrets of Coach Bazemore's success was the fact that every team in his feeder program—including the football teams in Valdosta's recreation department leagues—played football the Wildcat way. They used Bazemore's blocking and tackling techniques and drills and his offensive plays and defensive systems. The result was that, by the time a youngster was a sophomore trying out for the Wildcat varsity team, he likely had already played Wildcat-style football for six to eight years, and was nearly as familiar with the system as the coaches were.

You may not have that degree of influence or input in your particular situation, but it is doubtful that Bazemore had much control in *his* situation when he began, either. As his program caught on and captured the town's imagination and fancy, though, he was able to extend his influence to all levels of Valdosta's feeder program. It's something to consider, at least.

Through techniques such as those described previously, you can and should attempt to exert a positive influence on the coaches who comprise your feeder system, including urging them to devote considerable time and effort to teaching fundamental skills. If young athletes learn the basic skills properly at an early stage in their training, you will be relieved of the task of teaching those skills yourself or re-educating youngsters who learned them improperly, and you can thus spend your time refining and sharpening those skills rather than starting from the "Men (or Ladies), this is a (football, basketball, etc.)" phase.

4. Provide opportunities for recognizing young players coming up through your feeder program, but not the same recognition or rewards that your varsity players get. You can have a "recreation night" at one of your home games in which rec league or intramural players get in free when accompanied by their coaches or parents; introduce intramural or rec league champions at a varsity home game; or encourage media coverage of local feeder teams, to list three suggestions. What you should *not* do is invite players other than those on your jayvee and varsity teams to your sports banquet; single out for special praise in the media any individual players who are coming up through your feeder system; or reward your jayvee or B-team players as amply as you reward your varsity players.

Ideally, earning a spot on your varsity team should be the culmination of years of preparation by young athletes. They should consider it both an honor and a privilege to play for you and to wear the school colors of your varsity team. They *will* wear your uniform with pride if they have not received so much individual attention and recognition along the way that they now expect you to consider it an honor to coach them.

The apostle Paul considered moderation in all things to be a supreme virtue, and it is, at least when applied to the treatment of young athletes in your feeder program.

EIGHT POSITIVE CHARACTERISTICS TO LOOK FOR IN YOUNG PLAYERS

1. Players Who Listen

This point is number one on the list because it's an easily observable characteristic. Players must be willing and able to listen to their coach and to concentrate on what is being said. Anything we say is wasted on someone who isn't listening.*

---

*Because I'm hard of hearing myself, I should also point out that permanent hearing loss is not at all uncommon among young people. Partial deafness often is not diagnosed until years after it occurs, and as a result the hearing-impaired child may be mistakenly stereotyped by his teachers as a daydreamer, or by his coach as a poor listener.

Two hints for dealing with such a problem: first, the child probably is not aware that he cannot hear as well as other people, so it probably will do no good for you to ask him if he is hard of hearing; second, the best clue to his hearing loss is that he likely always talks loudly in order to make himself heard.

Before making any ultimate decisions concerning chronically inattentive players, you might consider talking to school personnel who are in a position to recommend hearing tests for the youngster.

2. Players Who Are Willing to Try New and Unfamiliar Skills Without Question or Complaint

We've all had our share of players who greet any new learning situation with the time-worn phrase, "I can't do that." My reaction to players with this kind of negative attitude is similar to the old Lucky Strikes cigarettes slogan, L.S./M.F.T.*: "Lord, Save Me From *Them.*

As has been noted previously, coaching is teaching. We can teach youngsters who are eager to learn. It's as simple as that.

3. Good Students

There are many advantages to coaching smart athletes. For example, we don't have to worry about their scholastic eligibility; we don't have to explain the same thing over and over to make ourselves understood; new and unfamiliar plays, patterns, and strategies are absorbed more quickly; and those athletes can be used to help other players learn their responsibilities more quickly.

4. Players Who Don't Like to Lose

Again, this is a relatively easily observed trait. All that is necessary is to set two players against each other in a competitive situation and observe how the loser reacts to failure or defeat.

In this regard, the coach should be aware that it is far easier to teach a fiery, intense, John McEnroe-type competitor to control himself than it is to teach a passive, mild-mannered player to play with abandon.

5. Players Who Are Loyal

Although vitally important to the growth of your pro-

---

*"Lucky Strikes/Means Fine Tobacco."

gram, this trait rates rather low on the list of player selection characteristics because, in most cases, it is not immediately observable.

Loyalty is not something that is turned on and off like a light switch; rather, it builds up over a period of time as the player's appreciation grows for the positive role that the team and the coach play in his or her life.

6.   Players Who Love to Practice and Play the Game

If a player is chronically late to practice; if he often misses practices entirely, with only the flimsiest of excuses for his absence; if he constantly asks how much longer practice will last; or if he consistently comes to practice or games without his equipment, shoes, etc.; it becomes rather obvious that the player does not like to practice and/or is not terribly concerned about his responsibilities to the team. And while punishment, suspension, or dismissal from the squad can solve the problem, the easiest way to deal with the problem is to warn players from the first day of practice that such behavior will not be tolerated, and then come down hard on the first violator—preferably before team selection is finalized.

Daily practice is a fact of life; whether a drudgery or a pleasure, it must be observed if players are to learn and improve. Skills are learned and perfected in practice (if at all), not in games. Players who cannot accept the hardships of repetitious drilling and rigorous conditioning in practice should be weeded out like crabgrass in the lawn, since the alternative—turning daily practice into a three-ring circus of fun and games—would seriously compromise team goals. This is not to say that practice sessions should never be fun or that they should not include drills or activities in which the players enjoy participating; indeed, such activities can relieve much of the tedium of long, exhausting daily practices. Still, it is we as coaches, and not our players, who should decide how long practices will last and how they shall be conducted. Players are not fired for losing games.

7. Natural Athletic Ability

In my experience, active in-school recruiting of, say, tall players for our basketball program is most important during the first year or two of coaching at a particular school, and tends to level off in importance after that.

When we first arrive at a school no one knows us. The students don't know what kind of person or coach we are or what we hope to accomplish, and they may have been turned off of athletics due to prior negative experiences with previous coaches.

In the beginning, we likely will have to spread the word ourselves, which means going to every potential athlete and urging him to take a chance on us and our program.

After we have been at the school for a while, though, word will get out via the student grapevine that we stand for certain principles and values, and we will tend to attract more and more ex-players and previously nonathletic students into our program who find us or our goals appealing. (This is, in fact, why many coaches always seem to have so many good athletes on hand: in addition to having developed a comprehensive feeder program to supply them with new potential athletes every year, they are able to retain those players by virture of the reputation and expectations they have established.)

Of course, we will still want to talk with every potential athlete in our school about trying out for our teams, since in some cases the problems (such as work, grades, etc.) which have prevented them from playing previously can be worked out to allow them to participate in athletics. Be warned, though: you don't want to waste too much of your valuable coaching time on an obviously lost cause. If you find five 240-pound high school boys in your school who have never played football before, you can bet your last buck that other coaches have tried diligently to get them out for football in the past, and with no more success than you're likely to have. You'll still try, or course, since you'd be a fool not to, but don't waste your time trying to persuade a kid to give up drugs, booze, or cigarettes and come out for your team. If he doesn't do it of his own accord, he'll never help your program.

Natural athletes and youngsters with body types that lend themselves to participation in certain sports are easily identified. My intention in placing this category near the end of the list was to remind the reader that, while athletic ability and body type are undeniably important, they may be overemphasized to the extent that other equally or more important factors may be overlooked. It is possible to become so hypnotized by a youngster's height, musculature, coordination, or quickness that we overlook other qualities that are necessary for that youngster or any other to contribute positively to the growth of our teams.

8. Leadership Ability

Leadership ranks last among the eight positive characteristics to be on the lookout for because of its relative rarity, not because it is any less desirable than the other characteristics. Every coach worth his or her salt understands the desirability of having effective team leaders. Whenever any player exhibits a desire to undertake a leadership role, that player should be encouraged and given ample opportunities to assume that role to the fullest extent possible. Many coaches feel that it is impossible to have too much leadership on your team, at least, not when that leadership exerts a positive influence.

And there's the rub, as Shakespeare said. We also have to be on the lookout for *negative* leadership qualities that can drain a team's morale and work against our efforts to build a positive, supportive atmosphere on our team. To use an old cliché, a few bad apples *can* spoil the whole bunch. And it's true, too, especially when those negative influences exert more leadership than the players with good attitudes.

Give Young Players a Chance

Actually, this last point is a coaching principle concerning not only player selection, but playing time as well. It is this: *with other factors being equal, give the nod to the younger player.* If, for example, you must choose, in filling out your squad, between a senior who cannot help you and an unskilled sophomore, go with the sophomore who will improve over the next three years through on-the-job training. (Of course, the reader will note that we said "with other factors being equal," which may or may not be the case in a given situation. And it is true, too, that you might keep the senior on the varsity team by placing the sophomore on the jayvee squad, but your decision should be based on what is best for your program, not on your reluctance to dismiss a player—especially a senior—during tryouts. If, in your opinion, the sophomore will benefit more from a year of jayvee competition than he would from varsity experience in which he would be mainly confined to the bench, only then is *that* the correct decision for you to make.)

WINNING TEACHING METHODS AND PRINCIPLES

1. Demonstrate. It is easier for a player to learn to execute a new and unfamiliar skill properly if he sees someone perform the skill correctly before attempting it himself. If you as a coach cannot perform the skill correctly and with proper form, perhaps you can find someone else who can do so—but *don't* try it yourself if you're going to look bad doing it.

In the absence of anyone who can execute the skill the way it should be done, you may be able to find films, videotapes, or even sequential or individual photographs that illustrate the action involved. Any or all of these resources are preferable to word descriptions alone.

Every skill should be demonstrated before it is practiced, if at all possible.

2. Communicate. In order to teach effectively, it is vital that we make ourselves understood. Demonstrating skills *shows* players what to do and how to do it—but that's only one-third of the problem. Another one-third consists of *telling* players what we want them to do and how they should do it. (The rest involves their learning by doing the skill.) And since verbal communication is not an exact science, breakdowns often occur between what we say and what our players understand. Thus, we must explain the same thing over and over, in different ways and terms, until we bridge the gap and understanding takes place.

We should be aware, too, that whenever a player does not understand what we've said, that player immediately becomes the weakest link in the chain as far as performing that particular skill is concerned.

3. Proceed only as far and as rapidly as your players are capable of proceeding without undue difficulty. Books are not read a chapter at a time, but page by page. Learning seldom takes place in rapid-fire, machine-gun manner; more often it occurs slowly, as players gradually absorb concepts that are new to them. And *that* is precisely why patience is not only a virtue, but a teaching necessity.

4. Break down complex plays or skills into smaller, bite-size components, and practice each component separately before putting them together. The simpler we make things, the more easily and quickly they will be understood and learned.

5. In teaching skills always stress using proper form and execution. Form and execution are the most important keys to consistency where skills are concerned. They are also vital to a team's overall chances for success. While it is not always necessary for players to use "perfect" form except in sports where form is graded (such as gymnastics and diving), they should be taught to at least approximate perfect form in the most important areas of the skill in question, such as using wrist flexion and extension in shooting a basketball to impart backspin to their shots.

How does a coach identify the most important areas of a given skill? By reading articles and books within his sports area that deal with teaching fundamental skills; by talking with other coaches and attending coaching clinics; and generally by the same methods he uses to acquire a broader understanding of any aspect of his sport or coaching, including analyzing the skills himself if and when he cannot find answers elsewhere.

6. Go through patterns and plays at a walking pace until the movements and actions are learned before attempting to perform them at normal speed.

7. When in doubt, go back to the basics. When a play breaks down, either return to walking speed to analyze the problem, or else go back and work on component drills.

8. Don't install a new system or adopt a new style of play unless you understand it thoroughly. You must understand it well enough to explain it to your players, answer whatever questions arise in the course of your explanation and subsequent practice of the new techniques, and make technical or tactical adjustments whenever necessary. Here are some guidelines concerning the addition of new plays, systems, or playing styles:

- When teaching players a new system, be positive about it.
- If it works, keep it.
- If it doesn't work, try a few simple adjustments. Often, the success of a play depends on its timing, in which case minor adjustments may bring eventual success.
- If it still doesn't work, forget it and try something else.

9. The "mental image" concept. Many successful coaches urge their players to form a mental picture of themselves performing a given skill before they actually perform it. Divers and gymnasts use this technique, and basketball players sometimes do, too, when they rehearse the movements in a free throw before the referee hands them the ball at the line.

A variation of this technique consists of videotaping the athlete in action, and then letting him study and critically evaluate his execution of the skill—with the coach's help, of course.

10.   Avoid letting daily practice sessions become a dull routine.   There are several ways to liven up the drudgery of long, tiring daily practices. The coach can vary the practice by adding new, challenging, and interesting drills; take time out from formal practice occasionally to do silly or unusual things, such as having ice cream or watermelon breaks, or weak-handed passing, shooting, kicking or batting contests, or "challenge" contests between players (or between players and coaches) in a spirit of fun rather than hard-nosed competition; or he can even give the team a day off from practice when the players are mentally and physically fatigued, as is often the case in the latter stages of the regular season.

You're the head coach. As such, you should know your players well enough to know when they need a change in their routine. And if you apply yourself to the problem, you'll come up with ways to keep your players alert and looking forward to your practices, no matter how long and hard the season has been.

TIPS
ON BUILDING
A CLOSELY KNIT
TEAM

I like to have a closely knit team. I like players to do things together off the court. And I like to show them I care about all their problems—their business careers, their love lives, racial situations, everything. I want them to know that they, and winning, come first.

—*Bob Cousy*

Together we shall achieve victory.

—*Gen. Dwight D. Eisenhower*

In entering a new coaching situation in which losing has become the expected outcome of competition, our goal of winning consistently will not be achieved until we have changed the attitudes and atmosphere in which players have grown used to losing. Because they are used to losing, they (and the student body as a whole) may not see any great and lasting values to be gained from being a part of our team. In such circumstances our initial goal should be, not winning consistently from the start, but rather *making our team and our program something positive and worthwhile that potentially gifted athletes will want to become a part of.* That's what this chapter is all about: tips on how to transform a group of individuals with separate (and sometimes conflicting) goals into a closely knit team of players who are unified and totally committed to our goals and objectives, whatever they may be.

LAYING THE GROUNDWORK FOR SUCCESS
AS A TEAM

1. Surround Yourself with Good People

If there is any sort of shortcut to long-term success in coaching, it is this: the more good people we are able to bring into (and retain in) our program, the more successful our program will be. (By "good people"; we mean, of course, people who will be loyal to us and our program.*)

---

*"The only 'bad' kid is the one who won't be loyal to his coach and his teammates." —Jerry Tarkanian

Just as a house must be built on a foundation of hard ground rather than soft sand if it is to withstand the ravages of time and the elements, so must an athletic program be based on the continuing, unswerving loyalty of those who operate within the program.

Loyalty is the bedrock upon which successful programs are built. And as every good coach knows, the process starts at the top and filters down; that is, in order to get the most out of our players, they must receive the best possible coaching. If you are a head coach with assistant coaches, one of your top priorities should be to see that good assistants are hired and retained—again, not only good in the sense of possessing knowledge of their sport, but in their enthusiasm for coaching and their loyalty to you, your program, and the players involved in it as well. (It goes without saying, of course, that the head coach owes a similar debt of loyalty to his players and assistant coaches.)

If forced to choose between having good *athletes* or good *people* on my teams, I'll take the good *people* every time! You can teach youngsters who have a positive attitude, and who listen to you and want to learn. They may not always win, but their loyalty to you and their devotion to the team will take much of the sting out of defeats. And when they win, you don't go to bed at night nagged by the feeling that you've sold your soul or compromised your principles for the sake of winning.

Having good people on your team will pay off in the long run, if not in the present, since their presence on your team will tend to attract *other* good people who may be potentially even better athletes.

Good athletes who feel no sense of loyalty to you or their teammates sometimes can provide you with wins, and thus with the illusion of progress as a team; what they cannot give you or your program is what you need most of all: *themselves.* And because they will not give of themselves beyond their own self-imposed limits, they'll let you and their teammates down sooner or later.

In the same sense that water seeks its own level, your

team's identity will be either positive or negative. In terms of building a solid foundation for future successes, it is *good people* (who may or may not be superior athletes) who will provide that all-important base of support without which you cannot long endure.

2. Strive to Create a Positive, Supportive Team Atmosphere

Expect and require players to accept their teammates without reservation, and to treat each other with respect. Be prepared to deal as forcefully as necessary with anyone who cannot adhere to this vital aspect of your philosophy.

According to head football coach Mike White of the University of Illinois, "The most important thing in a program is the attitude and atmosphere you create." Although every team is made up of individuals with diverse and unique personalities and backgrounds, everyone on the team must be made to understand that *the team's best interests always come first, before any thought of individual accomplishment or gratification.* Anyone who cannot accept this fact and act accordingly has no place on the team.

This is not to say, of course, that players must be "nice" to each other all the time; still, there must be a foundation of respect underlying the kidding that goes on constantly on all teams, or the result will be a team divided by ill will, dissension, and bitterness.*

When internal problems arise between teammates, they should be taken aside by the coach and given the opportunity to talk out their problem. They should be told why (and how) their attitude and behavior must change for the good of the team. If they cannot accept the necessity for attitude and behavior modification concerning their teammates, that is, if they continue to cause problems, they should be dismissed from the team.

---

*"If a house be divided against itself, that house cannot stand." —Mark 3:25

3. Stress the Team in Everything You Do

Let the players know in no uncertain terms that no one—not even the coach—is more important than the team. Every positive act performed by the coaches or players on the team's behalf is an additional building block in the cornerstone of success. Taken as a whole, such efforts promote positive morale and a sense of unity that cannot help but make the team and its individual members function more effectively in competition. Even when a team is losing more often than it might prefer to lose, a sense of "teamness"—or family—will yield positive expectations for future success.

4. Review All Team Rules at the Beginning of Preseason Practice

Try to keep the number of rules to a minimum, but stress that there will be no exceptions to the rules, no favoritism shown. Outline penalties in detail. Some coaches verbalize their rules; other coaches hand out mimeographed pages concerning team policies, procedures, and rules. It makes no difference which method you use, except that if you have a lot of rules you probably should have them written down for the players' benefit.

An excellent approach to the dual problems of rules enforcement and handling parental concerns about student grades was suggested to me recently by a veteran coach who understands the winning process as well as anyone. He suggested meeting with parents and players before the school year begins in order to go over with them the team rules concerning conduct, grades, and so on. At the meeting, he outlines his rules in detail, together with the punishments violators can expect to receive. Those rules, in essence, boil down to one simple set of absolutes that parents and athletes alike *must* accept in order for the athlete to remain associated with the program: *I am totally in charge of my program. I will be the sole judge of what is best for my program. I will not tolerate bad grades or bad behavior.*

No excuses will be accepted, he tells his audience. The student will be expected to perform to the best of his ability in every phase of his life. ("Our simple little rule," the coach says, is "All that you do, do with all your might, For things done by less are never done right.")

"I personally will not excuse a kid from any classroom to practice basketball or go to a game, etc.," the coach goes on. "Nor will I excuse my basketball player to go back to a classroom to take a test, make up missed work, etc. I think each player must have *full* responsibilities. If he needs to budget his time better, teach him. But don't give him an excuse. If you never say 'yes', you never have to say 'yes'."

After that preseason meeting, everyone concerned with the team knows exactly where the coach stands: his philosophy, his convictions, and what he expects in the way of student grades and behavior. As a result, he seldom encounters serious problems later concerning exceptions to the rules. And because his rules concerning grades are rigid, he never has to deal with the problem of parents removing their sons or daughters from his teams. They already know, via his preseason meeting, that he has their children's best interests at heart.

5. Outline Short-Term and Long-Range Goals for the Team

Tell players how you and they should expect to accomplish those goals. Army's head football coach, Jim Young, said, "Every program that I've gone into before—and I did the same thing at Army—I believe that you go in with the idea that you win immediately. Any time that you say it's going to take two or three years to build (a winning program), you're telling the players there at that time that they're not good enough to win. And you're not going to do it. So our plan (at Army) was to win the first year, and if not, then the second."

Still, if our short-term goals are unrealistically high in a losing season, the players are likely to become disillusioned as losses pile up, and they may not want to stick around to find out if our long-range goals are equally overly optimistic. That's why I believe that, if we don't have the horses, we should not create an atmosphere in which winning today's race is all-important.

If the importance of winning is not overemphasized in a losing situation, and if we explain to our players how our team goals will be achieved and offer evidence of continuing progress toward those goals, they will understand and accept the necessity of building skills on a short-term basis that will yield long-range successes in the future. After all, even in the worst of losing situations, players still want to win, although they may not possess the physical or mental skills to win at their present level of play. Our task as coaches is to convince them that working hard on a daily basis will produce positive results in the future, if not today.

6. Instill a Sense of Discipline in Your Players

Discipline is the willingness to make personal sacrifices for a cause because you accept the rightness of the cause. Everyone needs discipline, whether to provide order and direction in our lives (for example, meeting daily responsibilities) or to remind us that we act not only for ourselves, but for others who are affected by our actions as well.

In our modern age of broken homes, working parents and easy access to drugs, alcohol, and sex, it is *now*, more than ever before, that youngsters need to be exposed to the kind of strict discipline that the pursuit of team goals in athletics can afford when rigorously applied to their lives. In fact, we are hardly exaggerating at all in contending that athletics is one of the very few areas left in American life where young people are challenged daily to seek their personal limits of excellence. Certainly (with few exceptions) they are not challenged that way in the classroom or at home.

First you surround yourself with good people who will be loyal to you and to your cause. Then you teach them discipline by (a) transmitting to them a sense of urgency regarding their own roles in the team's fortunes, that is, by communicating to them that *they are most important to the team when they are giving 100% of themselves for the team;* (b) constantly driving them to the limits of their physical ability and endurance and challenging them not to back off or slow down until you reach the point where hard work and maximum effort at daily practices as well as in games are routine accomplishments; and (c) setting a proper example of self-discipline and commitment to the team and its goals yourself.

HOW TO BUILD THE TEAM CONCEPT

1. Improve Your Coach–Player Relationships

Take time to discuss players' personal problems with them privately, or just to talk informally with them. Encourage your players to come to you with their problems, and work with them to find meaningful solutions. Let your players know that what is important to them is important to you. Team unity begins with the relationship between individual players and the coach.

Our world has changed drastically in the years since Russia ushered in the Space Age with the launch of *Sputnik,* the world's first man-made satellite, in October 1957. And as life on earth has grown increasingly complex, growing up has become increasingly difficult in our rapidly expanding, rapidly changing society.

The day is long past when we as coaches can afford to ignore our players' personal problems and needs and maintain a strictly professional relationship with our players. To think otherwise is more than naive; it is *suicidal*—professionally, that is—when you stop to consider that, for example, any player on your team or mine can obtain virtually any illegal drug known to man if he or she so desires, and with a minimum of difficulty.

Taking time outside of your daily practices to communicate your concerns to players on an individual basis, and to listen to their concerns as well, can serve to forge powerful bonds of mutual respect, trust, and faith between player and coach. Even merely talking informally with players on a one-to-one basis about anything at all, whether important or trivial, reinforces this bond and enhances the player's self-image, since every player either openly or secretly covets the coach's attention and approval.

When players have personal problems, they seldom expect the coach or any other adult to understand those problems or spend a great deal of time working with them in finding solutions. And when we are willing to listen, understand, and help them, they usually are shocked, and then they are pleased and grateful to find an adult who cares about their problems.

The end result of such concern on the coach's part is players who are intensely loyal to him. And as has been pointed out frequently, loyalty is the bedrock underlying every successful sports program.

If I appear to overstate the case for communicating with our players on *their* level as well as *ours*, it is because when I was in high school, my basketball coach never had a kind or friendly word to say to me away from the court. As a result, I was terrified of the guy and was never able to relax in his presence, even in games.

In my own coaching, I'm up-tight and fiery—the sort of coach who needs a seat belt, strait jacket, and gag in his mouth to restrain him. My players understand and accept my volatile ways, though, because they know that it's just my game face, my way of dealing with the pressure. They understand this because I take considerable pains to explain it to them, both in informal, private chats and in talks with the team as a whole.

Away from practices and the pressure of game situations we should try to be relaxed and easygoing, especially in our dealings with our players. We should want them to know that, just as we expect them to go to war for the team's sake at practice and in games, we're behind them 100% in everything that affects their lives. For example, I want my players to know that, if tragedy struck and left them homeless, my wife and I would not hesitate to take them into our home and raise them as members of our family. And if I can satisfy my players that I'm telling them the truth in this regard, do you really believe I'll have trouble communicating anything else I want to get across to them?

That's why, in this book and others that I've written, I've placed considerable emphasis on the virtues of loving your players and being totally devoted to their well-being. The way I see it, if we don't like young people, and if we don't enjoy being around them, we're in the wrong profession. And if we *do* like them, we should *let them know it!* It may not be the macho thing to do, but it *works*—and it wins games, too!

Concerning listening to your players: your instructors may not have told you this in your college coaching courses, but part of your job as coach involves counseling confused youngsters who are involved in the agonizing process of growing up. Sometimes they need the reassurance of an understanding adult to listen to them, and there just aren't many adults in their lives who will take the time to listen to them and try to understand their problems from their point of view. If you are one of those few adults who takes the time to care, they'll appreciate it more than they'll ever tell you, but you'll see the results of that appreciation in their loyalty and willingness to go to war for you and the team.

It's important, too, for players to be made aware that they aren't the only ones who have problems. We—their coaches—face some pretty big problems ourselves, such as trying to win games every now and then in order to keep our jobs. And to the same extent that we are willing to go the proverbial extra mile to help our players come to grips with their problems, we have every right in the world to expect them to give their best efforts, not only for us but for the team as well, at daily practices as well as in games.

In this context, players should be made to understand that *the court or playing field is not the proper place to solve personal problems, and daily practice is not the proper time to address those problems.* One approach a coach might use in getting this point across to his or her players is to underscore the physical danger involved in letting one's attention stray from the task at hand (particularly if the sport is as physically demanding and violent as, say, football). At the same time, the player should be reminded that, while everyone has problems, growing up means possessing the maturity to wait for the proper time (in this case, after practice is concluded) to deal with, or seek help for, those problems. He should also be reminded of his responsibilities to his teammates, who are counting on him to fulfill his obligations to the team while practice or games are going on.

In other words, the player should be made to understand that the team and its goals and objectives take precedence over individual needs *while the team is working toward accomplishing its goals.* Individual personal problems cannot be permitted to assume equal or greater importance than team goals, regardless of how negatively those problems are perceived by the athlete in question. No one is more important than the team.

2. Praise Different Players from Time to Time

When you stop to think about it, our players don't really ask much of us. Oh, they may complain occasionally about how long or hard our practices are, but they rarely if ever draw up petitions to have us fired for not winning often enough. They seldom complain that we're not working hard enough on the team's behalf, even in situations in which such complaints might be justified. They appreciate our honesty, they expect fair treatment, and they expect us to attend daily practices and show up for games. Beyond those things though, our players tend to accept us for whatever kinds of coaches and people we are, for better or worse.

Still, our players deserve some kind of recognition or reward for the long hours of rigorous training we put them through and for the sacrifices they make in order to participate on our teams. And because they generally do not expect or demand such recognition, they are invariably proud and delighted to receive occasional compliments, praise, and kind words from their coaches. A warm smile that signifies friendship and acceptance, or a kindly pat on the back or verbal praise every now and then, may affect our players' morale to a greater extent than the promise of an undefeated season. Some coaches also make it a practice to convey to their players any complimentary remarks made about them by their teammates, teachers, classmates, or anyone else whose opinions they might appreciate. (But they do not pass on any comments of a negative or derogatory nature, except those regarding their schoolwork or behavior in class. What they don't know won't hurt them, or the team.)

Such actions on the coach's part tell each player on the team that he is important to the team and the coach. They signify the coach's acceptance and effectively communicate his concern for them both personally and as a player. Praise, compliments, and recognition always make people feel better about themselves; and when those people are our players, the team as a whole benefits.

We should note that the coach's praise often serves as subtle reinforcement in the sense that the player is being singled out for behavior that the coach finds acceptable; thus, it sometimes can be used effectively (in moderation) to encourage desirable (conforming) behaviors such as hustling every day at practice or spending extra time after practice working on skills—but only when applied to players who earnestly seek the coach's approval. Such praise always should be warranted—and it should be administered sparingly and judiciously; it loses its effectiveness if it is undeserved or if it becomes so routine and commonplace that every time the players come together as a group someone whispers, *"Who's gonna get the Goody Two-Shoes Award this time?"*

There are other reasons for carefully gauging the amount of praise received by individual players. First, they may be highly skilled players who do not need such praise to motivate them—or else their ability to perform the skill may not be affected by praise, such as sinking putts or free throws: in both cases the praise may be wasted, and simple *recognition* will suffice. Second, Murphy's Law indicates that, if you *ever* single out a player for praise, he'll foul up badly the very next time he performs any given skill. There's more to that statement than jest, too: some players tend to relax, either mentally or physically, whenever they receive praise—and on higher levels of play, the amount of slacking off necessary to adversely affect performance may be exceedingly slight. And third, there is the possibility that the player involved may start taking seriously all the nice things that are being said about him.

3. Socialize Together

Whenever possible, do things together as a team away from the gym or practice field. Consider such activities as eating lunch together in the cafeteria; having cookouts, spend-the-night parties, or swimming or beach parties; going to the movies together; or taking a trip to an amusement park. The team should be a "second family" to the players, and the family that plays together, stays together.

For some sports you can use money-making projects to raise funds to buy attractive travel outfits that will be an additional source of pride for team members.

4. Confront Problems Directly

Don't be afraid to confront problems directly, and don't expect them to go away as if by magic if you choose to ignore them. Virtually every major problem in life was once a minor problem that was not treated before it grew out of control.

When problems arise between players, the coach should act as a third party and have the players sit down and talk out their difficulties. The coach should not take sides at this point, but he should let the players know that the problem must be resolved *now*, and to the mutual satisfaction of all concerned—including him—before it becomes disruptive to team morale. In laying the groundwork for resolution of the problem, the coach should emphasize that their problem cannot be allowed to tear down the unity that everyone on the team is striving toward; that, while even family members often have disagreements, they don't stop loving each other; and that, if they care about each other and the team, they will want to solve their problem and put it behind them.

If the players have had sufficient time to resolve their problem but have reached no area of mutual agreement and reconciliation, the coach should be prepared to outline in detail how each player will be expected to behave in relation to the other in the future, and explain to both players the consequences of their failing to live up to his expectations in this regard.

Coaching is, in a very real sense, the art of solving problems on a group basis. The more deeply the coach applies himself to the solution of problems as they arise, the more likely he is to achieve positive results in his coaching. This is true whether we're referring to problems between players, or finding workable team patterns and plays for his team to run, or building and maintaining a winning program where none existed previously.

5. Publicize Your Team at Every Opportunity

If opportunities don't arise, create them. Media publicity in particular is both a reward for our players and an incentive to lure other, uninvolved students into our program.

Care should be taken to keep players from taking their publicity—especially individual attention in the media—too seriously. Overconfidence sometimes arises when players start believing the things that sportswriters and sportscasters are saying about them.

Where the coach **is** concerned, praise for individual stars should be balanced by emphasizing their roles within the team concept and by singling out the progress or achievements of lesser players for attention as well.

WINNING COACHING PRINCIPLES

In matters of principle, stand like a rock; in matters of taste, swim with the current.

—*Thomas Jefferson*

Nothing can bring you peace but the triumph of principles.

—*Ralph Waldo Emerson*

In this chapter we shall consider 25 principles of coaching that relate in one way or another to winning: 18 general principles and 7 technical, or tactical, principles.

Perhaps I should state at the outset that I did not devise these principles, nor do I necessarily accept or agree with every one of them. They have evolved over the years through the combined efforts and experiences of countless thousands of coaches.

GENERAL COACHING PRINCIPLES

1. Superior teams may be able to win with talent alone; lesser teams must rely more heavily on playing style and/or tactics.

If the other side is armed with cannons and automatic rifles and all we're using is BB guns, it shouldn't take a genius to figure out that pitting our strength against *their* strength isn't going to win us many battles. Yet how often we as coaches do just that—say, by trying to run with a superior fast-breaking basketball opponent, or by hammering into the middle, play after play, against a clearly superior opponent in football, in a futile effort to establish a power-oriented ground game. And when the game is over and our basketball team has lost by 45 points, or our football team has amassed all of 35 yards rushing and 50 yards in total offense, we shake our heads sadly and wonder what went wrong.

The truth is, we aren't likely to defeat obviously superior opponents at all, but the odds against us increase dramatically (and in some cases virtually to the point of impossibility) when we decide to play their game by attacking them where they are strongest. This does not include situations in which the opponents' superiority is due largely to the presence of one superstar-caliber player in the lineup; in such cases, much may be gained by going directly at that player—for example, by trying to get him in foul trouble in basketball or by forcing him to make quick and accurate decisions or else take himself out of the play, and reducing his pursuit of the play in football.

If victory is to be achieved against vastly superior opponents, it likely will result from finding and attacking their weaknesses, not their strengths, or adopting a playing style that tends to reduce the effectiveness of their playing style by upsetting the rhythm and tempo of their attack.

More will be said about these points in the latter part of this chapter. For now, though, let us remind ourselves that, if we intend to enter into mortal combat against a tiger, we had better come prepared with some pretty effective weapons in our arsenal.

2.   Winning is habit-forming; success breeds success.

The more often a team wins, the more confident players will become that they can and will win in the future. Along with that growing confidence will come an increasing willingness on their part to work ever harder in order to continue to win, simply because winning is more fulfilling than losing. It is also more fun.*

Such a revelation should come as no surprise to us. The ancient Roman poet Vergil wrote, "For they can conquer who believe they can." And in more modern times, Dr. Norman Vincent Peale, author of the best-selling book *The*

---

*"They laugh that win"—Shakespeare, *Othello*; and similarly, "Winning is like taking a vacation" —Sonja Henie, ice skater

Power of Positive Thinking, asserted that when you change your way of thinking, you change your world. It's all a matter of expectations—and positive expectations tend to yield positive results.

3. There are no shortcuts to success, no gains without pains.

These are old clichés, admittedly—but they also happen to be true, most of the time. The only real shortcut to success in coaching consists of inheriting a team filled with superstar athletes—and even then the problems of using those athletes to best advantage and keeping them happy and hungry can be enormous.

One should not embark upon a coaching career expecting to be blessed with superstar athletes and dynamite teams at every turn in the road. If you happen to inherit a powerful team, be grateful for it. But don't think that just because your team is strong the job will be easy. It never is. Getting the most out of our players is always a difficult and challenging task that demands the very best we have to give.

4. Over the long haul, winners work harder.*

Everyone wants to win, but the consistent winners are those who are consistently willing to pay the price of success.

Given superior athletes to work with, it probably is possible for a coach to win often without working very hard at it. But when those athletes are gone, whether due to graduation, scholastic ineligibility, or whatever reason, a coach's sins of omission eventually will catch up with him if he has not paid proper attention to the various elements involved in building a successful long-term program.

---

*"The harder you work, the harder it is to surrender." —Vince Lombardi

5.   You can (and should) drive a team harder when it is winning than when it is losing.

The adage that "winners never quit" is literally true: when players' expectations for winning are high, their willingness to pay the price of success will be high too, as will be the level of their refusal to quit short of victory. And if they refuse to give up in games, they also will refuse to give up when faced with increasingly demanding and challenging practices—within reason, of course.

The same may not be said of losing teams, however. When players are used to losing, they tend to give up earlier in games than if they expected to find a way to win. Their tolerance for pressure is likely to be low, whether they are facing pressure-filled game situations or rigorously demanding practices. If they are driven beyond the limits of their expectations, they will tend to give up in despair—which is precisely why they have adopted the mantle of *losers*. Care must be taken to *gradually* increase our expectations and demands upon them and to exercise great patience in our dealings with them, or else they will lose their desire to participate further in what for them is an extremely unhappy situation.

Bobby Jones of the Philadelphia 76ers once said, "Winning cuts the season about in half. When you're winning, the second half of the season doesn't seem nearly as long." And when you're losing, the season itself may seem to last an eternity.

6.   All good coaches are good teachers—or good recruiters, or both.

At the college level, at least, it is possible to be a good (but not a *great*) coach simply by virtue of recruiting superior athletes who will make the coach look good; at the high school level, a mediocre coach can achieve the same results if he inherits a strong team or an effective feeder program.

Beyond this, though, it is the day-to-day teaching of

fundamental skills that builds winning programs. The coach who hopes to rise above mediocrity on a regular basis will constantly search for new and better ways to teach effectively the skills associated with his sport. Good teachers never stop learning, and they will try virtually anything they can think of to increase the likelihood of learning taking place.

There's an old Japanese proverb that goes, "To teach is to learn." It relates to open-mindedness, a worthy virtue that every coach and player should possess, since it is open-mindedness and the desire for knowledge that make teaching and learning possible. As automotive pioneer Henry Ford said, "Anyone who stops learning is old, whether at twenty or eighty. Anyone who keeps learning stays young. The greatest thing in life is to keep your mind young."

Perhaps basketball's legendary John Wooden said it best, though: "It's what you learn after you know it all that counts." And that goes for coaches as well as players.

7. The successful coach identifies, recruits for, and/or develops to the fullest extent possible the most important physical skills and attributes in his or her sport.

Good pitchers—or quarterbacks, or point guards—don't grow on trees, and there's nowhere in the Yellow Pages that we're likely to find them.

Let's say that we're looking for pitching candidates for our baseball team. Likely, we'll begin our search by having everyone on the baseball team take turns pitching to see who may be able to fill the bill in terms of control and/or the ability to throw a hard fastball. (In the latter case, control can come later: to paraphrase Bobby Knight, we may be able to teach a youngster to control his fastball, but we will never teach him to throw it 90 m.p.h.) We may also scout physical education softball classes for other youngsters who can "fling that ol' apple," as Dizzy Dean used to say. And we may even resort to talking to other athletically built nonathletes that we see around the school campus, in hopes of getting them to try out for the baseball team. In each case, we're taking the important first steps of identifying the necessary skills and searching for candidates to meet our need.

After that, we begin the process of developing the available talent, which translates into teaching our pitcher candidates how to pitch.

The same holds true for every sport, and for every skill within that sport. It's a matter of identifying the skills needed, and then studying the available personnel to see who might best be able to fill the vacancy.

8. All successful coaches are good motivators.

Motivation is the art of getting people to perform necessary tasks that they might not do on their own. It includes (but is not confined to) encouragement, inspiration, and expectation.

As was stated in the Introduction, *everyone wants to win—but some people want to win more than others.* When players want to win so badly that we can almost *feel* the desire for victory flowing within them, no additional motivation may be necessary. Still, even the most highly motivated of individuals needs prodding somewhere along the way, and less highly motivated individuals may require constant motivation for them to do their best at all times.

The capable motivator constantly studies his players for signs that their concentration is lagging or that they are not putting forth the kind of effort that they are capable of giving. At the same time, because that coach has developed, by virtue of studying his players over a period of time, a feel for knowing which players need pushing and which ones need pulling, he usually is able to determine with some degree of accuracy the type and amount of motivation needed to achieve his goals.

Generally speaking, aggressive or extroverted personality types, such as effective team leaders or players who are confident in their ability to deal with situations as they arise, respond more favorably to pushing (prodding) than to pulling (encouragement). Although exceptions exist, confident players normally do not need continuing encouragement as much as they need to be reminded that they are *expected* to get the job done. That's what *pushing* is all about.

Pulling, on the other hand, normally is more effective when dealing with shy, passive personality types who lack confidence in themselves or who do not function well under pressure. With this sort of player, an approach which stresses that "You *can* do the job; I *believe* in you," is far more likely to be believed (or even heard, in some cases) than a more hard-line approach to motivation.

Motivation is an art, not an exact science. The best motivators recognize this fact, and as a result they are willing to take chances now and then, based on what they know about their players.* They seldom if ever take motivation for granted or assume that their players will be "up" for a given opponent. For the best motivators, motivational preparation is as integral a part of their overall game preparations as deciding what offenses and defenses they will use.

9. Among equals, the team that most wants to win (or expects to win), WILL win.

They'll find a way to win—and if none exists, they'll *create* a way to win. For teams who refuse to lose, the game truly "isn't over till it's over," in Yogi Berra's words.

The problem is to make sure that it's *your* team, and not the opponents' team, that most wants to win.

10. Among teams of nearly equal ability and skills, that one that makes the fewest crucial mistakes will win.

It is basic to the nature of coaches to want to be in con-

---

*When motivational attempts fail, as they often do, motivation means sometimes having to say you're sorry.

trol of situations at all times. Mistakes cause teams to lose control or to play out of control. This is why the majority of coaches are basically conservative in their approach to their chosen sport: they know that critical mistakes can defeat them, no matter how hard their players are trying. They know, too, that taking chances and performing high-risk skills (such as running triple-option plays or passing in football) drastically increase the probability of error, and thus the possibility of losing as well.

11.   Defeat is a state of mind.

You aren't truly defeated until you think you are.* The scoreboard says differently, of course, but scoreboards, like statistics, don't always reveal the whole truth. My team may have had to go into three overtime periods to defeat a clearly inferior opponent because I or my players were not properly prepared for the game—and I, for one, would consider our effort to be a losing one, not a victory. Or, my team gives a magnificent effort against a vastly superior opponent, only to lose on a lucky half-court shot at the final buzzer; in terms of what I expect from myself and my players, it's clearly a win for our side.

Winning, like love, can be a state of mind rather than a provable fact: if you think you're in love, you are; and if you have a winner's never-say-die attitude, and give a physical and mental effort worthy of winning, you *are* a winner where it counts: in your heart. This is true whether we're talking about a single game, or a season, or a career, or even a lifetime.

Unfortunately, the same may be said for *losing*.

Losing consistently is easy. It requires no effort beyond scaling the mental hurdle of admitting that we cannot win. Having made such an admission, however, we soon find that, in future confrontations, accepting defeat as inevitable becomes increasingly easy to do. The path to success is clut-

---

*"The loss which is unknown is no loss at all." —Publilius Syrus

tered with those unhappy souls who gave up somewhere along the way.

Thus, we try to teach our players not to accept defeats as final, but rather to regard them as momentary setbacks, or guides to show us how far we have to go. The wins show us how far we've come.

12. In order to win consistently, a team must be able to function normally in abnormal or pressure-filled situations.

While it is probably true that more games are lost due to critical mistakes than are won by last-second heroics, in either case winning is largely a matter of handling (or failing to handle) the pressure when the outcome is in the balance. (The "pressure" that we're referring to is, of course, the pressure to win, since no pressure to lose exists unless one has been paid to throw the game. Fear of losing and the pressure to win are two sides of the same coin.)

Taking the process a step further, we find that the pressure to win actually is no more or less than the ability to overcome fear by concentrating intently on the task at hand, or at least the ability to concentrate while one is afraid.*

Thus, we arrive at the crux of the matter: the ability to concentrate, whether in pressure situations or otherwise, is a learned skill. *We can teach our players to concentrate on what they're doing, even in tense, pressure-filled situations, by creating similar situations in practice.* (If you doubt this, tell your players that they can skip wind sprints at the end of practice today if they can, say, make ten consecutive free throws within a five-minute period. They may not succeed, of course, but in the process you may see levels of concentration from them that you never before knew they possessed. And while this technique probably is inferior to those described in Chapter 7 in increasing players' ability to

---

*"A hero is no braver than an ordinary man, but he is braver five minutes longer." —Ralph Waldo Emerson

concentrate under pressure, it exemplifies my point that we as coaches *can* positively influence and improve our players' ability to concentrate.)

13. Luck favors those who are prepared to take advantage of it when it occurs.

As someone once said, "You never know when opportunity is going to come knocking at your door—but there's nothing to prevent you from positioning yourself by the door where you'll be sure to hear the knock."

The best way to ensure that the breaks go our way is to teach our players to play alertly; that is, to teach them to concentrate on the action and their roles within it and to anticipate the unexpected. (That's why football and basketball coaches practice loose-ball drills.) Along with this, there's the factor of playing hard enough to create our own luck by forcing opponents to make mistakes. In many instances, what we call "luck" is simply a matter of alert players' taking advantage of mistakes.

14. You cannot win consistently without being organized in your coaching.

With all the tasks and responsibilities that a coaching position carries with it, there simply is no excuse for a coach's not being organized in his work. A house is not built without blueprints, nor a long trip undertaken without road maps and a final destination in mind.*

Organization is our means to ensure that what must be done, *is* done, and in the quickest and most efficient manner possible. The alternative to an organized approach to coaching is to act spontaneously, or to do whatever occurs to us as it occurs—and the result usually is *chaos*.

---

*"Our plans miscarry because they have no aim. When a man does not know what harbor he is making for, no wind is the right wind."—Seneca, a Roman statesman (4 B.C.–65 A.D.)

In one memorable example of disorganized coaching, a first-year coach suddenly realized on the morning of his first football game of the season that he had forgotten to send his player eligibility forms to the state high school association for approval. Unless he had the forms approved before the game began that night, his players would be ineligible and the school would be fined. The result was a frantic scramble to fill out the forms, followed by a hasty 300-mile trip to and from the state athletic office. The coach finally made his way back to the field house at 5:00 that afternoon, a nervous wreck and totally unprepared for the game that lay ahead.

The following year, the coach completed his football eligibility forms and mailed them to the state office on the first day of preseason practice.

15. Improvement is a full-time, year-round process, for coaches as well as athletes.

Let's put it this way: if your involvement in your sport is year-round, and mine ends with the final horn of the last game of the season, which of us likely will show more improvement in our coaching by the time next season rolls around?

I wrote the first of my eight published coaching books in 1974, after having endured a season in which, for a number of reasons, my basketball team did not accomplish what I felt we were capable of achieving. I wrote the book in the off-season as a means of improving my own understanding of the game.

In my estimation, at least, any day that a coach gives no thought to his team, his goals, or his sport is a wasted day.

During their courtship, Coach George Allen took his wife-to-be Etty out for dinner one evening. She was enchanted by the kisses (Xs) and hugs (Os) and Cupid's arrows (→) that George kept drawing all over his napkin, and she decided that he must love her very much. As it turned out, he did—and he does—love his wife very much, but that wasn't exactly the message that those Xs, Os, and arrows were meant to convey!

16. A game isn't won until it has been played.

This statement is true on three levels of interpretation. First, there's the fact that the only sports in which you win games with your mouth are Bingo and hog-calling. Second, there's the possible problem of overconfidence, which sometimes leads to upsets when players expect the opponents to bring a white flag of surrender with them for the coin toss or opening center jump. Third, we've all seen incredible, unbelievable late comebacks that either won games or almost won them. I can recall seeing a Dean Smith-coached University of North Carolina basketball team score seven points in the last 17 seconds of the game to come from six points down and win by one point.

In each case it is the coach's duty and responsibility to control his players, whether by monitoring their comments to the media or by constantly searching for ways to motivate them toward winning performances, even when the outcome apparently is not in doubt.*

17. Plays don't win games; players do.

No play, system of plays, or playing strategy will work without players who can make it work. Plays are designed to work, of course, but their success in any given situation depends on at least four factors: the players' skills; their confidence in the play, system, or strategy; their understanding of their roles; and their willingness to work hard enough to make the play work. To whatever extent the players are lacking in any or all of these categories, the re-

---

*Bear Bryant often stressed to his players the necessity of having what he called "good mamas and daddies" to raise them with proper respect for traditional values. Once, after a particularly convincing Crimson Tide win, an Alabama player was asked by a reporter why the opponents were defeated so soundly. "I guess, " the player replied, "they just don't have good mamas and daddies."

sults will be correspondingly less satisfactory than if no areas of weakness existed.

18. Girls want to win just as much as boys do.

If you have ever coached a girls' team, you probably already are aware of this. Girls and women who participate in athletics are not frail, dainty creatures who go to pieces in crisis situations and need constant rest and tender, loving care in the midst of physical exertion—and they don't respect a coach who treats them as if it were so. They are *athletes*, and they should be treated as such.

Of course, certain unique problems arise when coaching girls or women, but generally those problems can be alleviated by treating the players as athletes rather than as girls or women. Boys don't get pregnant or have menstrual cramps—but coaching girls can be as rewarding as coaching boys because, in our society, girls traditionally have not been expected to excel in sports. Thus, they are likely to respond positively to any coach who cares whether they excel. The challenge of excellence and winning in sports likely is a relatively new experience for them, and they tend to approach the task with a vigor and dedication that surprises many first-time girls' coaches.

Too, the fact that girls traditionally have been "allowed" to give vent to their emotions can work in the coach's favor, since they are likely to respond positively to a broad range of motivational approaches. So if you find yourself in a situation in which you are expected to coach a girls' or women's team, don't despair; give it your best shot by forgetting sex differences and coaching them as if you were coaching boys. They'll try your patience in a thousand ways—just as boys do—and some of them will look for excuses to get out of hard work now and then, the same way that boys do. But if they are truly athletes, they will respond to your coaching in a positive manner. They will strive to the best of their ability to achieve whatever short- and long-range goals you set for them, and they will do so with every bit as much enthusiasm as any boys' teams you've coached.

TECHNICAL (TACTICAL) COACHING PRINCIPLES

The following seven principles relate to coaching strategy. Where coaching strategy is concerned, few guarantees exist. The only universal law that applies to the use of strategy is likely to be Murphy's Law; namely, "Anything that can go wrong, *will* go wrong."

These tactical principles are based on playing the percentages, or improving or maintaining the odds in our favor. The prudent coach will use or disregard them as he thinks necessary in a given situation, keeping in mind, of course, that virtually every game situation is unique, and must be dealt with individually.

1. Never change a winning hand; always change unsuccessful tactics.

If you've been dealt a straight flush in a game of five-card draw poker, you don't want to throw away four cards in hopes of drawing four of a kind. In a similar vein, if what you're presently doing in a game situation is successful, change may be both unnecessary and undesirable.

On the other hand, if a play or tactic consistently fails to produce the desired results (or if a given player's performance is depressingly unsatisfactory), switching tactics or players may serve to reverse the trend, at least temporarily.

For example, most varieties of full-court pressing defenses in basketball are designed to force the ball away from certain players or toward certain predetermined areas of the court where the dribbler or pass receiver will be unable either to dribble past a pair of trapping defenders or to pass to a teammate. When the press works, usually it is because the elements of surprise and confusion have caused the ball handler to panic and throw the ball away or try to dribble through the trap.

However, when the opponents are able to anticipate the

trap and organize their attack; that is, when they are not surprised or confused when the trap is sprung, they may even be able to mount an effective fast break with numerical superiority of their own at the other end of the court, since the two trapping defenders are at least momentarily removed from the play.

That's why many basketball coaches don't always full-court press throughout games; it also explains why those same coaches are likely to vary their presses, using zone trapping some of the time; man-to-man, run-and-jump defense at other times; and operate from three-quarter and half-court as well as full-court alignments. Their goal may be, not to steal the ball or force a turnover every time, but to keep the opponents off balance and confused about what to expect. If one particular style of full-court pressing defense is working especially well, they may stay with it until the opponents figure out how to beat it, at which time they will switch to another full-court pressing tactic or otherwise vary their defense.

2. Don't experiment at crucial moments in games.

Of course, circumstances may dictate otherwise, but generally the place to experiment with new techniques, plays, and tactics is at practice, where players can listen and learn in a relatively pressure-free environment. Once they have learned to execute the skill, play, and so forth with proper timing, precision, and confidence in practice, they should be ready to perform the same skill in the pressure cooker of game situations. How well they execute the skill in critical game situations depends upon how well they respond to pressure, of course—but trying to teach new and untried techniques, plays or tactics to players during a one-minute timeout at a critical moment in the game, with the bands booming and cheerleaders and fans shouting themselves hoarse, is hardly likely to ease the pressure or help the players to concentrate on the task at hand.

3. Play to negate opponents' strengths or to take advantage of their weaknesses.

This strategy is basic to all sports; it is *vital* for teams whose personnel is inferior to that of their opponents.

If a team has weaknesses—and all but the very best of teams have weaknesses, however slight—we may be able to discover ways to attack those weaknesses through diligent study of scouting reports and/or game films, talking with other coaches, and the like. Such efforts may not always pay off in victories for our team, but they can serve to reduce the odds against us and give our team its best chance to compete against superior opponents on relatively equal terms.

Let us briefly consider ways to deal with six commonly encountered areas of weakness which even the strongest of teams may fall prey to: overdependence on the performance of one outstanding player, depth problems, the presence of inexperienced players in the lineup, lack of quickness, injured players in the lineup, and flaws in skills execution.

Overdependence on the performance of one outstanding player. If the opponents' success is due largely to one highly skilled player, we may be able to reduce their overall effectiveness by controlling that player (for instance, by double-teaming or fronting him in basketball to keep the ball away from him or by assigning one or more players to key on him on every play in football) and thus forcing the rest of the team to beat us. Sometimes, superior players become frustrated when they are consistently taken out of the action and deprived of doing what they do best. Beyond that consideration, though, the player in question may tire quickly from having to work harder than he is used to working, in which case he may lose his incentive to continue to give 100 percent on every play.

In basketball, a player's effectiveness may be sharply curtailed by getting him in early foul trouble. (A coaching acquaintance tells me that this is, in fact, his favorite technique for dealing with the sort of superstar-oriented team that we're discussing here. He explains, "If the opponents have an outstanding big man, we'll go inside, directly at him, *every time down court*, until he picks up enough fouls to force him out of the game. He may block ten shots in the process, but he won't block any more shots while he's on the bench. And when he comes back later, we'll do it all over again, until he either fouls out or gives up trying to block our shots.")

Other techniques for dealing with superstar-oriented teams might include pitching around the opponents' batting superstar (that is, walking him intentionally) when the rest of the lineup is weak offensively; forcing a big man in basketball to play an up-tempo, full-court game that will not permit him the luxury of resting or relaxing on defense (which may succeed if he's slow and relatively immobile, and if our team fast breaks effectively, but probably will not work if the opponents' fast break is better than ours); changing strategy whenever the superstar is on the bench resting, in order to take full advantage of his absence; or simply playing the superstar normally and concentrating our efforts mainly on stopping the rest of the team.

Regarding the latter point, many basketball coaches don't accept the notion that one player can beat you. Their feeling is that, if he's good enough, he'll probably get his points anyway, so you are likely to achieve better results by giving him his 40 or 45 points and trying to hold his teammates' scoring to a minimum. And while not everyone subscribes wholeheartedly to this viewpoint—it certainly does not apply equally well to other sports, such as football, where an outstanding I-back or quarterback *can* beat you—it can serve in basketball to keep your own best players out of serious foul trouble.

Powerful teams that are short on depth. The key here is to make the opponents work hard enough for their starters to require rest periods on the bench, or, in basketball, to get them into foul trouble. Of course, this strategy is far from ideal, since the opponents may be in great physical condition—and if they're good enough, they may beat us soundly before they even begin to tire.

In basketball, relentless movement, fast breaking, and aggressive man-to-man defense sometimes can serve to tire opponents by making them work harder than they normally do. The task is more difficult in football, since controlling defenders means controlling the ball offensively through a series of long, sustained drives, and then shutting down their offense before their defenders have time to rest and catch their breath.

At any rate, the purpose of this strategy is to attack whatever weaknesses are to be found in the opponents' lineup when some or all of their starters are out of the game.

The presence of inexperienced players in the lineup. Inexperienced players often can be intimidated by rough physical play of the sort that the Los Angeles Raiders or Georgetown Hoyas are noted for, and because they are inexperienced, such players may not function well in pressure situations. In the former case, attacking them early in the game may discourage them from giving their best effort, and in the latter case, directing our attack at them late in games may cause them to make crucial errors of the sort that lose games.

Lack of quickness.   In the opinion of UNLV head basketball coach Jerry Tarkanian, *quickness*—not height or vertical jumping ability—is the single most important physical attribute in basketball.* And while the point is open to debate, there's no denying that quickness never hurts a team except when it is the opponents rather than we who have it.

If the opponents are slow afoot, their other advantages may be greatly reduced if they are forced into situations in which quickness is mandatory, such as defending the triple-option play in football or playing a high-tempo, fast-

---

*"Jerry Tarkanian and William Warren. "The Role of Quickness in Basketball," *The Athletic Journal*, Vol. 60, No. 3 (November 1979).

breaking game in basketball. As Coach Tarkanian has pointed out, it doesn't matter if a guy is eight feet tall, he isn't going to block shots if he's at the other end of the court when an opponent is shooting a layup.

Incidentally, this strategy—playing to negate opponents' strengths—is also known as *playing against your opponents' tempo*: if they play fast, *we* play slow, or vice versa. It is used in situations in which the opponents are clearly superior to your team, for the purpose of taking them out of their preferred playing tempo and making them play the game at *our* speed. The farther players are taken from the way they prefer to play, the more likely they are to make mistakes that they would not otherwise have made.

Players who are playing even though ill or injured. The object here is not to further aggravate the player's injury, but rather to take advantage of his injured state by directing play toward him. If, for example, he is a defensive back with an injured ankle, his reduced mobility may make him a prime target for our passing attack. Such a strategy is no more unethical on our part than his own coach's decision to play him when he is unable to play at full speed.

Flaws in skills execution. Even highly skilled athletes sometimes develop flaws in their play that an observant coach can take advantage of. In football, for example, linemen or quarterbacks sometimes use a slightly different stance on pass plays than on running plays in order to get an extra-fast start in dropping back. In baseball, pitchers sometimes tip off their pitches by their delivery motion, or by the manner in which they hold the ball in their gloves. And in basketball, even the pros often bring the ball down to their waist or below in gathering themselves for leaping slam dunks. (In the latter case, one wonders why defenders bother to go up and try to block the shot at all—and thus foul the shooter in the process—when all they have to do is reach out and grab the ball while it's at waist level or below.)

4. Play to accentuate your strengths and hide your weaknesses.

This strategy is best applied by a team that is clearly superior to its opponent.

When he was coaching at UCLA, John Wooden seldom if ever bothered to scout his opponents. He preferred to make opponents play the game *his* way and at *his* tempo by using his players' strengths to maximum advantage. When his players were short and quick, as was the case with his 1963–64 squad, which went 30–0 and won UCLA its first NCAA basketball championship, he won largely by virtue of a fierce, relentless full-court pressing defense. Later, when he had dominating big men like Lew Alcindor (now Kareem Abdul-Jabbar) and Bill Walton prowling the paint at both ends of the court, he combined fast breaking with an awesome inside power game to overwhelm most opponents.

In order to accentuate our strengths, we must first identify them, and then find a way to play toward them as often as possible. This usually is not too difficult a task when we are blessed with outstanding players; still, it is well to remember that two notions of "strength" exist: first there are the *coach's* strengths, namely, those phases of the game that he best understands or believes in; and second, there are the *players'* strengths, which may or may not be used to best advantage in a given style of play.

Thus, the question sometimes arises, *should a coach adapt his players to his system or style of play, or should he adopt a style of play that utilizes his players' strengths to maximum advantage?*

What happens when the players adapt to the coach's strengths? The most important consideration here is the coach's philosophy. A coach must be true to his basic philosophy of how he feels the game should be played, including the elements he feels are most important in terms of winning. Beyond that, he is limited only by the extent of his understanding of the sport.

Most coaches are basically either defensive- or offensive-minded; that is, they believe that one or the other phase of the game is more important in terms of producing victories. With a limited number of hours allotted to practice in the course of a season, many coaches tend to devote a majority of their time and efforts to either defense or offense, depending upon which phase they consider more vital to winning (and, in some cases, depending upon which phase they feel more comfortable coaching).

In order to understand the value of adapting players to a given style of play, one has only to consider the "Lombardi sweep" used by the Green Bay Packers under Vince Lombardi's tutelage; or the "guard-around" offense used by Kentucky Wildcat basketball teams under Adolph Rupp and Joe. B. Hall for more than half a century; or the four-corner delay game used so successfully by Dean Smith's UNC Tarheels until the NCAA added a shot clock. In each case, the style became associated with the coach to the extent that there was never any question of changing what had been proven effective over so long a period of time.

The greatest advantages of this concept of adapting players to a given style of play are that (a) the coach is able to teach more effectively because he believes in, understands, and is comfortable with the style of play that he is teaching; (b) once the style is learned, it becomes almost second nature to the players, who understand it so thoroughly that errors in execution are minimized; (c) the college coach can recruit players to fill specific needs and the high school coach can accomplish the same objective through an effective feeder program—and in both cases players know beforehand what to expect from the coach and the style of play; and (d) because the style does not change appreciably from year to year, carry-over value is high: returning veterans do not have to undergo any kind of lengthy learning periods.

The weakness of this concept is that, in certain cases,

the coach's preferred playing style may waste the talents of
superior players, such as a Herschel Walker–type running
back operating in a wishbone offense, or a Dan Marino–type
quarterback handing off the ball on virtually every play in a
"three-yards-and-a-cloud-of-dust" running attack, who
would be more effective in another style of play.

**What happens when the coach adapts to the players'
strengths?** Playing to our players' strengths refers not to
letting players do whatever they want to do, but rather to
searching for ways to use our players' strengths to best advantage and as often as possible. While it is true that a coach
should coach what he knows best, he should also be flexible
enough in his thinking to adapt or alter his team's playing
style to take full advantage of individual players' unique
skills or abilities.

Concerning the allotment of practice time, many basketball coaches feel that more time should be spent in shor-
ing up one's weaknesses than on practicing one's strengths.
And while their point is well taken, I've always tried to win
with my strengths rather than trying to avoid losing by
virtue of my weaknesses. Translated into allotment of practice time, this means that I prefer to spend a majority of my
basketball practice time ensuring that my team's strengths
remain strong enough to win for me. My reasoning is that,
since only a limited amount of practice time is available, I'd
rather spend as much time as possible improving what my
players do best.

I'm basically a defensive-minded basketball coach. In a
given season, I expect to spend 85 percent of my time working to build a solid defense, because I believe that defense
wins basketball games. And because I'm defense-oriented,
my teams generally have been better defensively than offensively.

Still, whenever I've had strong offensive teams, I've
tried to devote as much time to offensive basketball as to defense. In such cases, I feel that I'd be wasting time if I spent
85 percent of my daily practices working to shore up a de-

fense that will eventually let me down in games anyway. Thus, I'll cut down my 85–15 defensive ratio to, say, a 50–50 split between defense and offense, which gives me 35 percent more time to work on keeping my offensive strengths at full potency.

Naturally, I don't expect every coach who reads this to agree with my rather unusual theory of practice time allotment. Still, it's worked for me over the years, and it's something to consider. If your offense is weak, you'd better have a very good defense, or vice versa, or else you're going to lose a lot of games and waste a lot of time and energy on nonessentials in the process. ("Nonessentials" are those aspects of our players' performance that aren't going to improve appreciably no matter how much we practice them.)

How to hide your team's weaknesses. Although virtually every team has weaknesses of one sort or another, strong teams' weaknesses may not be readily apparent because their strengths are so overwhelming that opponents never get a chance to find and attack their weaknesses. If your team's strengths cannot adequately compensate for its weaknesses, there are a number of techniques you can use to hide them.

For example, let's say that your basketball team relies rather heavily on the performance of a superior offensive player who has just picked up his third foul with 6:30 remaining in the first half. Your instinctive reaction may be to take him out of the game for the remainder of the half in order to avoid risking his picking up his fourth, and possibly fifth, foul. In doing so, though, you risk falling so far behind the opponents that you will not be able to catch up when your star returns to the court in the second half.

Rather than benching him for the last 6:30 of the half, you might want to consider "hiding" him defensively by altering your defensive matchups to have him guard a weak offensive player, or else switch to zone defense and place him where he is unlikely to pick up a defensive foul. One coach tells me that on his team, whoever is in foul trouble automatically moves to the point in his 1-2-2 zone defense, with instructions not to block shots, attempt to steal the ball, or otherwise play defense aggressively. His team defense is weakened somewhat by this strategy, he says, but no more so than if the player in question were warming the bench, and his continued presence in the lineup gives the team offensive firepower that would not be available if he were doing "pine time."

Of course, the possibility exists that such a player may pick up an offensive foul or two somewhere along the way, but he may *not*, too, in which case your gamble is likely to pay off handsomely. It's a risk you'll have to consider when the time comes. Most coaches probably wouldn't want to take this sort of gamble, but sometimes desperate circumstances require desperate measures.

When he was coaching football at tiny Toombs Central High School (average daily attendance: 114), Coach Stan Scarborough never had the luxury of 11 quality football players on his team. In order to partially hide his offensive weaknesses, he used a shuttle system of nonathletic wide receivers' going long on every play to occupy part of the defense, which had to honor the wide receivers' routes or else run the risk of giving up the long bomb. (This is called a "run-off" technique.)

Defensively, Coach Scarborough used Jerry Claiborne's wide-tackle six alignment, which gave him eight players to defend against running plays. Of course, with only three defensive backs in the lineup, his teams were rather vulnerable to passing attacks, but he reasoned (correctly) that most of the quarterbacks his teams faced were not good enough passers to defeat him, and that, over the long haul, he was more likely to be defeated by his opponents' overpowering running attacks if he used conventional Oklahoma 5-2 defense.

Because he had virtually no effective pass blocking, his quarterbacks used a three-step drop and quick passes (especially to the tight end) to loosen the defense, or else they used screen passes or sprint-out patterns and short passes to receivers flooding an area. He also used a tight wishbone running attack with the fullback aligned 18 inches behind the quarterback in order to prevent quick penetration by the linebackers or interior linemen, to jam up the middle, and to give the linebackers less time to pursue the play at the corners.

Other ways of hiding weaknesses in football might include the following: (a) using fold- and trap-blocking techniques rather than trying to overpower defensive linemen; (b) using less-skilled players at positions such as down linemen, and placing your better defensive athletes at linebacker, defensive end, and strong safety; (c) stacking your linebackers so they cannot be blocked as effectively; (d) shooting the down linemen on every play, such as by slanting, to confuse blocking assignments; and (e) aligning your linebackers five yards deep (as opposed to, say, aligning them two yards off the line of scrimmage). Concerning the latter point, the linebackers' penetration will be reduced, but the offensive linemen attempting to block them will, in effect, be required to execute difficult open-field blocks to take them out of the play. Your linebackers will then have to be quick enough athletes to elude such blocking.*

It is important, too, to re-evaluate ourselves, our teams, and our individual players periodically during the course of the season as well as during the off-season or preseason. The overall complexion of the team tends to change somewhat during the season, as starting lineups are altered by injuries, players develop unexpectedly (or fail to develop as expected), confidence levels rise or fall, and so on. What started out as strengths sometimes wind up as weaknesses, and vice versa.

Some coaches hire professional scouting firms to scout their own teams at various points during the season, thus

---

*Thanks to Mr. Tommy Dyke, principal of McIntosh County High School in Darien, GA, and ex-head football coach at Tryon (GA) Academy, for his invaluable assistance with this section.

obtaining an unbiased analysis of their strengths, weaknesses, and what their teams are doing as opposed to what
they might be doing with the available players. Lacking
funds to hire a professional scouting concern, a coach might
instead ask a local retired coach, or even one of his ex-
players, to scout his team, say, one third or midway through
the season. Sometimes a new set of eyes looking objectively
at our team can spot nuances of team or individual play that
we have thus far overlooked, and which, when identified,
will permit us to alter our playing style in small ways that
may help us.

5.   The winning team is the one that is able to control the tempo of the game.

Enough has already been said previously about controlling the tempo of games that little more discussion
should be necessary, except to remind the reader that "controlling the tempo" means playing the game at our pace, and
dictating when and where confrontations occur. If we have
a strong team, we should be able to dictate the tempo most
of the time by playing to our strengths. If, on the other hand,
our team is weaker than our opponents', we should try to
control the tempo by attacking the opponents' weaknesses
or using a playing style that contrasts with their normal,
preferred playing tempo.

6.   If you give a team enough opportunities to make mistakes, it probably will make them.

Two football coaches who were practitioners of this
philosophy were Alabama's Bear Bryant and Georgia Tech's
Bobby Dodd. Between 1958 and 1964, these two great
coaches conducted some epic football battles that consisted
mainly of hard-nosed defense and offensive maneuvering
for field position as each team waited for the other to make a
critical mistake. Quick-kicks on first or second down were

common occurrences, and generally the team that won was the one that was able to cash in on the opponents' mistakes.

Of course, this was at the tail end of the era of one-platoon football, when talented players still played both offense and defense and fatigue was a greater factor than it is today, but the principle still applies: mistakes lose games, and the more mistakes a team makes, the more effectively it will have to play in other phases of the game in order to overcome the adverse effects of those mistakes.

7. Opponents who are not defeated convincingly are not defeated at all.

This does not mean, of course, that we must demolish a hapless football opponent by a score of 86–0 in order to establish our superiority over them. What it means is that, if we call off the troops and send in our third-teamers before victory is assured, we may not win at all. Stranger things have happened. The possibility always exists that the elusive "momentum" that television sportscasters like to talk about will swing to the other team when it achieves success against our scrubs, and then when our starters return to the court or playing field, they may be emotionally flat, overconfident, and/or physically stale from having cooled off on the bench or sideline.

Thus we arrive at what I call "Warren's First Law of Bench Coaching"; namely, *do what is necessary to win the game.* Apply the knockout punch whenever the opportunity presents itself, lest the opportunity never come again.

As has been noted, mistakes can beat you. I believe it is a mistake to give opponents a chance to come back and defeat you when you have a valid chance to put the game out of reach.

We've all seen boxers get an opponent in trouble, only to adopt the strange and unexpected tactic of standing back and letting the dazed opponent recollect his wits and his composure to the point that he fights back and eventually wins the bout. One wonders why a boxer would want to give his opponent such an opportunity when victory is clearly within his grasp. One thing is sure though: the very best boxers—those of the quality of Larry Holmes, Muhammad Ali, and Sugar Ray Leonard—never give their opponents that chance. They may fight sluggishly or erratically on occasion, but when the opponent is hurt, they finish him off as quickly as possible. As ex-heavyweight champ Joe Frazier explained, "There's one thing I don't ever think about: losing . . . . Instead, I think about how I'm going to win, and how I can do it the quickest way."

WINNING COACHING TECHNIQUES

chapter **7**

Study to show thyself approved, a workman
that needeth not to be ashamed.

—2 Timothy 2:15

The only way to win is to work at it.

—*Earl Anthony, pro bowler*

Sweat plus sacrifice equals success.

—*Charles O. Finley, ex-major-league
baseball owner*

The material in this chapter is divided into three categories, including six general coaching techniques, five points concerning preparation for games, and nine suggestions for dealing with game situations.

SIX GENERAL COACHING TECHNIQUES

1. Practice Counts

Stress concentrating and doing things right in practice as well as in games.* Admittedly, practice is not always fun. It can't be, not with the concentrated running, conditioning drills, and other physical demands necessary to prepare players for the rigors of competition. Still, there is much to be said for the contention that *athletes who truly love their sport look forward to daily practices.*

Players who would rather be doing something else besides practicing their sport, whether in informal, "backyard" fashion or in formal daily practice, are terribly misguided in their values. If their enjoyment of the sport can be turned on and off at will like a faucet, they don't really love the sport at all. (The same may be said for coaches, too, of course.)

Thus, it's important for us as coaches to explain to our players why practice is important, even though we may

---

*"You don't do things right once in a while. You do them right all the time."—Vince Lombardi

think that they already know why. Practice is where skills are learned and improved through constant repetition.

The same occurs in games, of course, but games cannot be stopped to correct errors and provide repetitive drills designed to overcome those errors. Practice affords opportunities to deal with problems of execution that cannot be attended to in the competitive heat of games.

If we expect players to do things right in games, the best way to ensure positive results is to train them to do things right in practice. Correcting errors as they occur; demonstrating techniques; and providing repetitive drills in skills execution are all tools of the trade for the coach who *teaches*. Almost equally important, though, is the coach's attitude toward mistakes in judgment and skills execution. If we *never* allow mistakes to go unnoticed and uncorrected, however minor those mistakes may be; if we carefully analyze for our players' benefit how mistakes arise and how they may be corrected; if we acknowledge our own mistakes and by our actions show that we are attempting to correct them; and if our own level of concentration and attention to detail during daily practices is as perfect as we can muster—then our players will accept for themselves the necessity of learning to do things correctly. They will learn to take pride in their performances, and their concentration levels will increase accordingly. As one coach explained to his players, "If you care about what you're doing, you'll concentrate on doing it correctly. *My* job is to see that you care."

If we want to improve our players' concentration, whether in terms of intense concentration over a short period of time or constant concentration over a lengthy span of time, we must first provide a suitable example for them. We should permit nothing short of the gym or field house catching fire to interrupt our practices. (Other exceptions: thunderstorms (if we're outside), tornado warnings, and injuries to players. Telephone calls can be monitored for urgency by team managers. One coach, wanting to show his players how important he considered his daily practices to be, had one of his assistant coaches burst out of the coaches' office shouting "Coach, it's the governor on the phone! He wants to talk to you!" The coach looked at his watch and shook his head. "Tell him to call back at 6:30. Practice will be over by then.")

Short-term concentration. Short-term concentration is far more easily achieved than concentration for long, continuous periods of time. So it follows that the teaching of short-term concentration should precede attempts to teach players to concentrate for an extended time.

If your goal is to intensify your players' concentration over a short period of time, you should incorporate some type of system of rewards and punishments into the various drills you use; in either case, the "payoffs" should be administered immediately upon successful completion or failure of the skill or activity. Psychologists are generally agreed that the promise of rewards is superior to the threat of punishment as a teaching and learning tool, since punishment teaches us to avoid certain actions but does not teach us what actions should be taken in order to achieve success. However, this fact does not mean that the threat of punishment cannot be used effectively as a teaching device, or that players should always be rewarded rather than punished. Short-term concentration may be improved through the development and use of competitive drills that carry the immediate promise or threat of reward or punishment. These are referred to as *self-motivating drills*, since the participants are virtually impelled toward high levels of physical output and quality of performance, regardless of whether they are normally attentive or highly motivated in their play.

Long-term concentration. Once players have been trained to concentrate for short periods, they should be ready to concentrate for longer periods at a time. This is done by moving gradually from drills of relatively short duration—say, virtually any simple individual or dual drill or competitive activity—to team drills of increasing complexity and lengthened time spans. Common elements to all such drills are these: they should be competitive; they should involve rewards and/or punishments; and they should provide objective evaluation of success or failure to the greatest extent possible. To the extent that these elements are present, the players will be virtually forced to concentrate on the task at hand, and without the necessity of the coach's acting as a cheerleader to spur them on toward greater efforts. If the rewards or punishments are sufficiently enticing, the players will motivate each other toward success.

Before leaving this topic, one further aspect of reward and punishment as applied to coaching and athletics should be noted.

Admittedly, the promise of rewards can be a powerful motivating force; still, the coach should be aware that, unless he is careful in structuring his drills, the players may consider other, unforeseen "rewards" to be more desirable than the reward he is dangling before their noses. For example, the promise of an additional water break for hustling may be less desirable to some players than the fact that they will be less tired if they give less than a full effort, particularly if the drill is physically demanding.

That is precisely why such drills must be competitive, and why they should involve both rewards and punishments if at all possible, if they are to achieve the desired results. Human nature dictates that most people tend to seek the line of least resistance whenever possible. If we as coaches desire to psychologically condition our players to give their best effort at all times, we must take this natural tendency into account in structuring learning situations. We can and should offer the carrot as often as possible, but we should also be prepared to use the stick occasionally.

2. Define Players' Roles Clearly

The more clearly a player and his teammates understand what is and what is not expected of him in competition, the more likely he is to accomplish the tasks assigned to him, and the less likely his teammates will be to blame him for his failure to carry out tasks that have not been assigned to him. Confusion concerning individual responsibilities is thus eliminated, or at least it is reduced drastically—and confusion loses ball games.

Perhaps no better example exists in sports of the necessity for defining and delimiting individual roles more clearly than that of the defensive end's responsibilities in coverage of the triple-option play in football. His responsibilities are simple: he is the contain man who must turn the option play inside by covering the pitch back on every option play. He also is responsible for covering reverses and counter-option plays run in his direction. If the defensive end does his job correctly, he will make few tackles, but will eliminate the trailing back as a wide threat. If he makes a mistake in this regard—that is, if he decides to go after the quarterback at the corner rather than staying outside to cover the pitch back—he risks giving the opponents an easy touchdown if the pitch is made, since no one else is even remotely available to cover the pitch back's wide route.

Each player should be made aware, via game plans and team meetings involving chalkboard sessions, of both his own individual responsibilities and those of everyone else on the team. This is not to say that every player necessarily should understand everyone else's responsibilities to the extent that he could assume any other player's role if necessary, but he should at least understand his teammates' roles as they affect his own particular role and responsibilities.

3. Share the Credit for Wins; Accept Responsibility for Losses

Considered separately, such actions tend to reveal the nature and extent of a coach's "classiness," since humility in victory and forthright leadership in defeat may define what others consider to be a "class act."

Considered together as two sides of the same coin,

these acts serve to build powerful bonds of gratitude, loyalty, and respect on the part of assistant coaches and players. In the former case, sharing the credit acknowledges that victory is achieved through the efforts of many people working individually on behalf of the team, and in the latter instance, the head coach's accepting responsibility for defeat eases pressure and directs blame away from other individuals who might otherwise have been blamed for the defeat. And just as no single play ever wins or loses a game, so it is also true that no one player—or coach—ever wins or loses games in team sports. For every "critical" play or coaching decision made in the waning moments of a close game, countless earlier "critical" plays and decisions were made, both successfully and unsuccessfully, which led to the present situation. Reverse any or all of those earlier outcomes, and the decision as to who wins and who loses likely would be no longer in doubt. (The prudent coach will carefully explain this fact to his players, hoping to teach them that *any given play, even one that occurs in the first minute of the game, may eventually turn out to be the "game-winning" play, although we won't know it at the time. That's why its important for each of us to give 100 percent on every play. If we want to win games, we must be ready to win whenever the opportunity presents itself.*)

Ultimately, though, it's just a matter of taking pains to give credit where credit is due in the case of winning, and taking the heat of public or peer disapproval off players where losing is concerned.

On the other hand, we should *never* allow our players or assistants to blame anyone, whether us, themselves, their teammates, or the game officials, for losses. Fans and boosters may freely blame anyone they wish, and whenever they wish to; that is their right as free citizens in a democracy. Team members do not have similar rights, simply because their roles and responsibilities disqualify them for that task. Team membership is not a democratic situation. If it were, preseason tryouts would be unnecessary. Players, assistants, managers, and other team personnel do not have the

right to express opinions that run counter to the best interests of the team of the individuals on the team. The line between *blaming* and *alibi-ing* can be exceedingly fine; both
are generally counterproductive to the pursuit and achievement of team goals. Even head coaches are well advised to
exercise their authority in this regard with extreme caution.

4. Don't Be Afraid of Overcoaching Your Team

If you *must* worry, let it be about *undercoaching* your
team. (By overcoaching, we mean that the coach's insist-
ence on following a predetermined, patterned style of play
sometimes tends to restrict players' ability to freelance or
use their individual judgment when improvisation may be
necessary.)

Television announcers and other media persons often
speak of overcoaching in negative terms, as if it were a
mortal sin ever to restrict players from "doing their own
thing." Don't believe it for a second. Virtually every great
coach in the business is an "over-coach"—or at least tries to
be. Dean Smith of UNC, John Thompson of Georgetown,
Richard "Digger" Phelps of Notre Dame, and Indiana's Bob
Knight are excellent "over-coaches," whose players function within the team role for them in college basketball,
only to routinely soar to unbelievable heights of individual
achievement in the NBA. Obviously, overcoaching never
hurt Adrian Dantley, Patrick Ewing, Bob McAdoo, Walter
Davis, Scott May, Uwe Blab, Isiah Thomas, Charlie Scott, or
Phil Ford (to name a few alumni of the aforementioned
coaches), and it won't hurt our players, either. While it *is*
possible to overcoach our teams, our greatest concern
should be to avoid giving our players too little coaching.

Overcoaching may occasionally lose games—depending upon your point of view concerning the coach's role in
winning and losing—but you can bet the second mortgage
on your house that undercoaching your team will lose
infinitely more games for you in the long run. It is far better
to risk overpreparing your players for games than to have

them enter competition with inadequate planning and preparation.

If you don't believe it, ask Coaches Phelps, Knight,
Thompson, and Smith: between 1975 and 1986, their basketball teams ranked sixteenth, fourteenth, fifth, and first,
respectively, in winning percentage in the NCAA.

5. Expect Your Athletes to Be Students, Too

Any other approach amounts to putting the cart before
the horse. Every student's first goal should be to receive a
quality education that develops him or her as a total person.
Athletes are *people*, not Os and Xs put on earth for the express purpose of catching passes or hitting home runs. We
can and must communicate our concern for our players'
scholastic development by demanding from them the kind
of effort in the classroom that we expect them to give on the
gridiron, court, or baseball diamond.

If we fail in this regard, we can expect to see other outside parties taking steps to ensure that "student–athletes"
achieve proper balance. Indeed, at least three states—
California, Texas, and Georgia—have already upped the
ante concerning minimum scholastic standards for high
school athletic eligibility. Other states will no doubt follow.
And painful as it may be for us to admit it, we as coaches are
to blame for the situation because, in far too many cases, we
paid lip service to our players' educational needs until
other governing agencies (such as state senates, boards of
education, and high school athletic associations) were
compelled, whether rightly or wrongly, to enter the picture
and dictate strict standards of educational achievement as
the basis for all high school athletic participation.

6. Always Be Positive in Your Statements to the Media

Even weaknesses should be presented in a positive
manner, if at all. Never belittle anyone, whether friend or

foe, in your public or private comments to any media person. The late Adolph Rupp used to regularly roast his own players in his post-game comments on his radio show, but he never described his opponents in any but the most positive of terms. If, like Coach Rupp, you've won four national titles and more than 800 games in your sport, you probably can get away with criticizing your players' performances publicly, but even then you shouldn't do it unless you can name even one positive outcome to be derived from it.

Where the media are concerned, our best course of action is to treat all of our comments as public, even when the interviewer swears on his grandparents' graves that what we're saying is strictly off the record.

Several reasons exist why we should never say anything negative about our opponents, even after we have beaten them. First, we may have to play them again in the future. Second, if we've beaten them, we don't need to rub it in. The victory should speak for itself. Being generous in victory or defeat is the classy thing to do. And third, calling a defeated team "a bunch of losers" may satisfy certain inner urges, but it also can take the luster off an otherwise-impressive win by suggesting that anyone could do what our team has done.

PREPARATION FOR GAMES

1. Develop a Plan for Winning

In school, we studied for upcoming exams—most of the time. And if we observed the results we achieved, we likely found a correlation between the amount of time we spent preparing for tests and the grades we eventually received. In coaching, the same correlation holds true. Our games are our tests. And as Bear Bryant astutely observed, his final exams were held every Saturday afternoon in the fall before 80,000 people.

Winning consistently is not an accident. Going through

an entire season undefeated is not a matter of luck, although luck certainly plays a part in winning games. As we have seen, the best teams—those that win, and win, and win—are those that are prepared to take advantage of lucky breaks when they occur and to minimize the effects of chance whenever it swings in the other team's favor.

From a coaching standpoint, winning consistently involves three factors: planning, preparation, and contingency. First, the coach develops a philosophy of his sport which reflects his views of how winning is achieved. At the same time, he evaluates his program to determine the actions and steps necessary to improve it. Such plans are necessarily broader than the specific preparations he will make to win games.

Second, the coach begins to train and prepare his players to perform in such a manner that they will win games as often as possible. These preparations—teaching skills; finding and adopting playing styles that will best complement players' unique abilities while hiding their weaknesses; communicating expectations; teaching strategies; and preparing and using daily practice schedules, scouting reports, and game plans—are virtually a never-ending process. They are the nuts and bolts that are necessary to build winning programs. They are the common denominators of the coaching task, the keys to winning the battles that eventually win the wars.

Third, the coach develops, to the best of his ability with regard for his players' skills and knowledge of the game, contingency plans for dealing with specific game situations. In basketball, for example, there are bring-in plays to be learned and rehearsed, tip-off plays, and plays to set up last-second shots.

Beyond these, however, there are the contingencies common to *all* sports: the games in which our carefully devised game plans aren't worth the paper they're written on. Every coach and every team experiences such nights when the best-laid plans just don't seem to work in the manner that they are designed to, but many coaches prepare for these in advance by devising alternative game plans to give their team an additional fighting chance to win.

The key to this process is contained in the words "what if?" What if things don't go as planned? What if my best player doesn't show up for the game? What if the opponents shut off our triple-option play? What if our basket has a lid on it tonight? What if our ace pitcher can't find the strike zone with a magnifying glass? What then, Coach?

The weak coach never even considers such possibilities until they occur. The average coach may consider the possibility, but shrugs it off by hoping it doesn't happen. The outstanding coach not only considers such possibilities, but also studies them to find ways of dealing with them should they arise. It's all a matter of paying attention to detail—but in the final analysis, it's what separates the men and women from the boys and girls where coaching is concerned.

How does one become such a careful, thorough coach where game preparations are concerned? It's easy. Ask yourself, whenever you consider *any* play, pattern, or style of play that your team is using or might use, "what could possibly go wrong?" Give careful thought to what you're presently doing or planning to do, in terms of how the opponents or Fate might upset your plans, and develop alternate ways of dealing with the problem. Another way to look at the situation is to reverse it and ask yourself, "If my opponents were using this play, pattern, or style of play against my team, how would I deal with it?" You'll find the answers if you search long and hard enough. And the extra work is never wasted, because it constantly broadens and deepens your understanding of the game.

Admittedly, the concept of straying from one's original game plan is controversial, and the farther one strays, the greater the risks involved. Any change from your original intentions entails risk, since the players likely will perceive the modifications negatively. Still, every coach makes adjustments in his game plan now and then, since if what we're presently doing isn't working, our only two options are to make changes, whether major or minor, in our style of play or our personnel (and thus give our offense or defense a new look that might upset the opponents' momentum), or else to continue with what we're presently doing that isn't working. Timeouts sometimes also can serve to slow down opponents' momentum by upsetting the flow of the action when the opponents are controlling the action—but timeouts are seldom effective in this regard when the opponents have already solved our offense or defense.

At any rate, a coach should be familiar enough with his offenses and defenses to make adjustments when necessary, and the time to begin considering such adjustments is before the game begins, by asking ourselves the simple question, "What could possibly go wrong with our plans?"

2. Look for Winning Edges

By "winning edges" we mean small details that can serve to create advantages where none existed otherwise.

Pitching around outstanding hitters can provide a winning edge in baseball. So can fouling poor free-throw shooting opponents when you're behind late in the game in basketball. Or directing the action toward tired or injured opponents in *any* sport.

The winning edges may be found if you're looking for them, and if you're prepared to take advantage of them.

3. Know the Rules of Your Sport

Play by the rules, but use them in your favor whenever possible. This advice should be a must for all coaches. Yet referees, umpires, and other sports officials I've talked with over the years constantly profess their amazement at how many coaches neither understand nor even are aware of many of the rules governing the sports they coach.

Rules in all sports are constantly being revised and updated. If we understand the rules thoroughly, we also by inference understand what is *not* covered by the rules, and thus we can sometimes take advantage of the shortcomings of the rule book.

Wright Bazemore, whose Valdosta (GA) High School football teams won nearly 300 games between 1942 and 1971, used to study the rule book for ways to use the rules (or lack of them) in his teams' favor. His search led to such innovative plays as the center sneak and lining up 14 or more players on the field for offensive plays.

Regarding the latter, just before the snap the extra players—wide receivers and blockers—would step off the field and onto the sideline, but the defense, not knowing which set of wide-aligned players were going to stay on the field and which were going to leave, had to exaggerate their defensive spread in order to cover both sides of the field, or else give up the easy touchdown via a quick lateral pass. Of course, covering six or more wide players tended to leave the opponents undermanned in the middle of the field, but as Coach Bazemore was quick to point out, neither the center sneak nor the 14-player alignment was illegal. (Both strategies are illegal now, thanks to innovators like Coach Bazemore who used the rules to their advantage.)

Most trick plays are, in fact, invented by coaches who take time to study the rule book.

4.   Don't Try a New Play Until You Understand It Thoroughly

If we're guilty in this regard, we'll likely find ourselves wasting valuable practice time solving problems that should have been solved before practice began. And until *we* understand what we're doing, we cannot realistically expect our players to understand or gain confidence in what we're doing, no matter how great it looks on paper.

5.   Discourage Your Athletes from Indulging in Potentially Dangerous Activities

While some activities such as drag racing or doing wheelies or other stunts on motorcycles or three-wheelers are highly dangerous and should be strongly discouraged, players also should be reminded that even apparently harmless horseplay sometimes can end up in serious injury.

Atlanta Braves pitcher Cecil Upshaw was walking under a storefront awning one day when he decided to show a teammate that he could still leap well enough to dunk a basketball as he had been able to do back in his college days. He went up to "jam" the imaginary basketball, and in the process he caught one of the fingers of his pitching hand in the awning. Upshaw narrowly avoided losing the finger.

Beyond even these sorts of activities, though, I think it's important to discourage our athletes from playing in informal pickup games involving nonathletes. Athletes are far less likely to get hurt when playing against superior athletes who perform skills correctly than when facing clumsy, unskilled, uncoordinated nonathletes who cannot perform skills correctly.

Athletes tend to play to each other's rhythms; that is, they attune themselves to the flow of their opponents' and teammates' movements, which are more or less predictable in most cases. Nonathletes, however, tend to be erratic in their movements. Seldom if ever are they predictable enough in their skills execution for the athlete to know when to get out of their way in order to avoid accidental collisions.

I have chronic neck and upper back problems because, in a pickup basketball game 14 years ago, a clumsy ninth-grader ran under me as I went up for a rebound. I flipped backward in the air and landed on my neck. The boy didn't mean to hurt me, of course; he was just trying, in his awkward way, to move into position to get the rebound that I was after. But that's precisely the point being stressed here: the nonathlete isn't trying to hurt our athlete, either—but he will, if our athlete gets in his way. He'll jab our player in the eye while reaching for the ball; or he'll hit him in the face with an errant pass or an errant elbow; or he'll step into the airborne athlete's path, not because he's trying to draw a charging foul, but *because he doesn't know any better.* The result is likely to be injury, recuperation, and lost playing time for our athlete. And it could be avoided by the simple expedient of teaching our players to avoid such situations.

If the Fates decree that our players are to be injured in competition, let it be during our formal practices or in the heat of games—not in meaningless pickup games involving our players and non-athletes.

DEALING WITH GAME SITUATIONS

1. Be Positive and Confident

When it comes to game preparations, I'm basically a worrier; that is, I try to anticipate the worst that can happen and prepare accordingly. I never use the same game plan from game to game because the problems facing our team are different in every game. I want my game plans to represent the very best effort that I am capable of giving on behalf of my team. It's the least I can do, if I expect my players to give *their* best efforts toward winning.

Prepare a game plan. Normally it takes me about three hours to prepare a game plan. I use a variety of colored felt-tip markers or highlighter pens to underscore or otherwise emphasize various points in the game plan. It makes the finished game plan attractive, eye-catching, and easy to read. I carefully erase or white out all errors, because I want the game plan to look as professional and workmanlike as the performance I expect from my players. An attractive, error-free game plan is a subtle reminder to my players that all of us are working toward quality in performance. I could not achieve this goal with a sloppy, hastily prepared game plan.

As I said, I'm a worrier. But when the game plan is finished and ready to be presented to the team, my attitude changes. If I have worked hard preparing myself and my players for the game, I am confident that my game plan gives our team its best chance for winning, and equally confident that my players will give a maximum effort toward winning.

I expect every player to study the game plan and scouting reports individually before I present them to the team. Later, when I go over the game plan with the team, I also discuss each player's specific role and responsibilities before the entire team, so there will be no misunderstanding as to what each player is or is not expected to do. After the team segment of the meeting is over, I go to each player individually and offer encouragement and suggestions or reminders as to how the player can best perform his particular responsibilities, analyzing the one-on-one matchups and clues from scouting reports.

Maintain a positive attitude. Every coach should fully understand, and believe strongly in, the merits of a positive attitude. He should want his players to expect to win. They should have confidence in the game plan he has devised, and they will, if he has properly conveyed his own confidence in its merits. Beyond winning expectations, though, the players must believe that their teammates and the coach cares about whether they give a total effort on the team's behalf in the upcoming game. They must feel that giving less than their best effort hurts people who honestly care about them. This, even more than being confident of winning, is what having a positive attitude is all about.

Deal with the fear. Confidence and a positive attitude are vital to success in sports, especially in those critical moments in which victory or defeat are on the line. At such times, a coach's greatest enemy is likely to be fear: the fear that a costly mistake will allow victory to slip through your fingers. And while every coach deals with this problem in his own way, three guidelines may be useful to the coach whose players have trouble conquering their fear.

Never let victory or defeat appear to rest on one individual's shoulders. One play never wins or loses a game in *any* sport; if it did, games would last only five seconds or so.

In a basketball game one of my players was on the free throw line for a 1-if-1 opportunity with 0:01 showing on the clock and the score tied. The player, an inexperienced freshman, already was 0-for-12 from the line that night. The opposing coach rightly called a timeout to increase the pressure on our hapless shooter. I told the player, "I know you're probably worried, but you shouldn't be. You won't win this game by yourself if you make the shot, and you won't lose it if you miss. Whether you make this free throw or not, we'll still love you tomorrow."

As it turned out, the player missed the shot and we eventually lost the game in double overtime. Neither I nor any of the player's teammates was ever heard to lay the blame for the defeat at that player's feet. I wouldn't allow it to happen, any more than I'd allow them to blame me or themselves. In team sports, one player (or coach) never wins or loses a game; to think otherwise is not healthy or productive for team morale.

"When the going gets tough, the tough get going." Controlled anger or aggression can be an effective, powerful antidote to fear. Neuromuscular skills may let us down in pressure situations, but playing harder and more aggressively can, in many instances, compensate for the increased tension that is present in do-or-die situations. And it can serve to create mistakes on the part of the opponents, who should be experiencing much of the same pressure themselves in those critical moments.

In such situations, you might want to remind your players of how hard they have worked, both in practice and in the game as well, to get where they are. After all, this—the opportunity to win—is precisely why they have worked so hard. Do they want to slack off now, when winning is in their grasp? Or do they want to work even harder than before to claim the victory that is rightfully theirs? Common sense should tell them that giving their all for a few seconds or minutes more is the only way that victory will be achieved.

Use humor to ease the tension of do-or-die situations. In an important high school basketball game of the sort that was described previously—no time showing on the clock and a so-so shooter on the line with the chance to win the game—the players huddled expectantly around the coach during timeout. He looked up at the shooter, frowned, and said to him, "Jeez, Freddy, back up a step or two! You've got bad breath!" The players cracked up and fell all over themselves laughing, including the shooter. The tension was broken, and the shooter later went out and calmly sank both shots.

2. Listen to Your Assistant Coaches, but Remember That the Responsibility for Final Decisions Is Yours

If you decide to take an assistant coach's advice in a given situation, or if you allow him to formulate the strategy for that situation, you should avoid the temptation to second-guess him when his strategy fails. (Better still, you should make it policy never to allow anyone associated with the team to second-guess game decisions after the fact.) And when your assistant coaches' strategies succeed, you should publicly acknowledge that fact, along with expressing your gratitude for their hard work.

A question that sometimes nags head coaches is, When should I make decisions myself, and when should I follow my assistant coach's advice? A good answer has been provided by Dr. Laurence Peter: "If you can tell the difference between good and bad advice (in a given situation), you don't need it at all."

3. If Possible, Reserve a Timeout

Whether used for discussing strategy with players or for resting tired players without taking them out of the lineup, timeouts are coaching tools. They should not be used frivolously. They should be saved for situations in which their need is clearly indicated. Other points to consider regarding timeouts:

- The coach should be aware of whether he is allotted a specific number of timeouts per half in his sport, such as football, or whether unused timeouts may be carried over to the second half of the game, as in basketball.

- Before calling timeout, it is sometimes advisable to see if the opposing coach is trying to signal for his players to call a timeout. If he is, you can save a timeout by letting the other team call it instead. It happens more often than you'd think, and you may be able to save three or four timeouts over the course of a season that you might otherwise have wasted.

- Be organized during timeouts. If you seem composed and organized in your thoughts, you will also appear to be confident that things will work out all right, and your confidence will be transmitted to your players.

- If you have one or more assistant coaches, you might want to confer with them briefly before huddling with the players. In addition to discussing possible strategies, you can use these few seconds to compose yourself and collect your thoughts. If you don't have an assistant coach, you can instruct the managers to pass out towels and water, and then stand apart from the players for a few seconds while you calm yourself or organize your thoughts.

Use phrases. Having decided what to tell your players, you might want to consider using brief phrases—no more than two or three words, repeated several times for emphasis. After all, you have only 45 to 50 seconds to talk to them, and there's no time for long-winded speeches. Besides, brief phrases are more easily remembered that complete sentences.

An outstanding high school basketball coach was instructing his team during a timeout. He was telling his players to play hard-nosed man-to-man defense that way he had taught them to. This was how it went: "Stay down (in their defensive stances). *Stay down!* (Louder the second time, for emphasis.) *Ball pressure! Deny* (all passes)! *V-front* (the post player)! *V-front, Robbie! Quick feet! Quick feet! Quick feet!*"

And that was it. It may not read well, but his players knew what he meant. As he talked, he switched his gaze from player to player, jabbing his index finger at them or into the air or his palm for added emphasis.

The coach later explained that, when he first tried this technique, he used four- to five-word phrases. As he found ways to simplify his instructions, he gradually reduced the phrases to one to two words each.

Did it work? the coach was Pete Aycock, and in his seven years at Appling County High School in Baxley, GA, his Pirates averaged 21 wins per season (and 85 points per game as well). And when Draughon Junior College in Savannah, GA, decided to organize a basketball team for the first time in 1984–85, Aycock was named head coach. His team won its first 25 games that season.

While many factors doubtless account for Coach Aycock's success in coaching, he considers the use of short, emphatically delivered, easily remembered phrases to be his most effective game-situation coaching tool. (He is quick to point out, too, that a coach need not wait for timeouts to use the phrases; in fact, he first used such phrases in live-ball situations in which his players could not give him their undivided attention, but could hear and respond to brief instructions called out by the coach.)

Finally, while many coaches already use such tactics from the sidelines, Coach Aycock brings two new wrinkles to the technique: first, he uses the phrases during timeouts as well as live-ball situations; and second, he always uses the same phrases in the same circumstances. (Concerning the latter point, he has compiled a list of one- and two-word phrases to cover every aspect of his offenses and defenses.

He uses them in teaching situations in daily practices, and he drills recognition in game situations by using them in full-court scrimmages. He teaches his players to respond to his voice above crowd noises by shouting appropriate phrases from the sidelines while cassette tapes of rock music are being played at full volume.)

4. Physical Contact Among Teammates

Physical contact among teammates (such as holding hands) can be a powerful motivator when exercised in game situations such as huddles in football and timeouts in basketball. The contact serves as a subtle, yet constant reminder to each player of the bonds that tie them together as a team.

Some players—especially boys who have been conditioned against such behavior in our society—may at first display reluctance to hold their teammates' hands, thinking it unmanly; but such reluctance usually vanishes rapidly, especially when the coach points out that many pro football teams hold hands in their offensive and defensive huddles, and no one ever accused the likes of Mean Joe Greene of being unmanly.

5. Have Bench-warmers Play an Active Supporting Role

Some coaches like to have their bench-warmers and substitutes stand up and applaud whenever a teammate leaves the game and joins them on the sidelines. Such gestures of respect tell the player that his efforts on the court or playing field are appreciated, whether or not those efforts were ultimately successful. And when he knows in his heart that he has *not* performed well, the applause and a handshake or two from his teammates show him (and the spectators as well) that they have not lost faith in him.

6. Don't Antagonize the Officials

Don't make them look bad. If you do, they'll hold it against you, and either consciously or subconsciously they'll tend to call against your team. I speak from experience here, since over the years I've been a notorious referee-baiter. My justification is that I expect the game officials to work as hard in their jobs as I do in mine; after all, on a per-hour basis they're getting paid a lot more for officiating than I am for coaching. Still, the end result has been, in far too many instances, a costly handicap for my players that could have been avoided if I had exercised greater self-control in my dealings with officials.

7. Don't Antagonize Opponents

Don't antagonize superior opponents who aren't playing well—and *never* antagonize *any* opponent before the game. "Let sleeping dogs lie," the saying goes—and with good reason. If the opponents aren't playing well—for example, if they aren't up for the game mentally or physically—they may not awaken from their lethargy at all, or at least until it's too late for them to mount a winning effort. But if we or our players arouse them by taunting, fighting, or other means, we're liable to find out exactly how well they can play when they put their minds to it.

That's why the media always feature dull pre-game interviews in which opposing coaches and players take turns describing each other in terms of such a glowing, complimentary nature that even a mother would be embarrassed. No coach worth his salt is going to risk baring his soul to a reporter concerning an upcoming game. If we were to tell a reporter what we *really* think, our words would be posted on every locker and wall in the opponents' dressing room. And, like as not, we'd find ourselves eating those words before long.

8. Never Give Up

Enough has been (and will be) said in this book about the positive values to be derived from maintaining a never-say-die attitude that it hardly bears mentioning at this point. The coach's game behavior absolutely *must* reflect his belief that every second of every game is important, regardless of the score, who is ahead, or who is in the lineup. It must, that is, if he wishes to instill a similar attitude on the part of his players. As George Eliot once wrote, "Any coward can fight a battle when he's sure of winning; but give me the man who has pluck to fight when he's sure of losing."

Examples of refusing to give up in hopeless situations include calling timeouts in the latter stages of negative blowouts to reinforce in the players' minds the importance of concentration and playing under control in *all* situations; using the remaining playing time to try out new plays or strategies that have been performed in practice but not yet used in games; or providing additional playing time for inexperienced players, with the clear understanding that you are doing so for their benefit, and *not* because the balance of the game does not matter. (Concerning the latter point, some coaches prefer not to "clear the bench," but rather to keep, say, 40 percent of the starters in the game to provide continuity and a semblance of leadership.)

9. Give Substitutes Playing Time

In basketball, the more important the game, the more important it is for you to give your first-line substitutes some playing time, however slight, before critical moments arise. "First-line" substitutes may be second-stringers or whoever is likely to see playing time in the game. You may be, like the University of Kentucky's legendary Adolph Rupp, the sort of coach who believes in going with his starters most of the time. Even so, you should be aware that it is always easier for substitutes to adapt to game conditions quickly when they are entering the game for the second time. They will still feel the pressure of critical situations, of course, but not to the same extent as when they are entering the game for the first time under such circumstances.

It is seldom desirable to bring a player off the bench cold to perform complex neuromuscular skills in pressure situations, since the player must adjust to the pressure of the situation. Still, if such a situation cannot be avoided— for example, if our quarterback is injured or our point guard fouls out of the game—we should instruct the substitute to use basic techniques (such as calling one or two running plays involving simple handoffs in football, or using protective ball-handling techniques in basketball) until he is able to adjust physically and mentally to the game situation and begins to relax in his playing role. Then, and only then, should he be instructed or allowed to use his skills to aggressively attack the opponents.

In other words, it is usually unwise for a cold, untested second-string quarterback to begin passing immediately in tense situations, or for a basketball player to shoot or attempt high-risk passes or dribbling techniques before his muscles have loosened up. Normally, players require no more than a play or two in football, or one or two team possessions in basketball, for them to warm up, lose their butterflies, and get into the flow of the game.

THE WINNING FORMULA: A TEN-POINT PROGRAM FOR SUCCESS IN COACHING

chapter **8**

Success is simply a matter of luck. Ask any failure.

—*Earl Wilson, columnist*

The toughest thing about success is that you've got to keep on being a success.

—*Irving Berlin, songwriter*

Game coaching is no more than the tip of the iceberg, the highly observable 7 percent of the coaching task. The rest—the other 93 percent—is what takes up most of a coach's time and energy. Without proper attention to that "other" 93 percent, game coaching becomes rather futile and meaningless.

—*Bill Warren*

Recently I watched a segment of the *NFL's Best Ever* television series that was devoted to the late Vince Lombardi. I listened to all-pro Willie Davis saying that "Coach Lombardi used some of his players to get across his message to the team—we were 'Lombardi people,' " and all-Pro Jerry Kramer saying that "Coach Lombardi liked to think that the difference between us (the Packers) and other players wasn't physical, but a matter of character. Coach Lombardi molded character." And as I listened, I realized that what I was hearing was exactly what I've been writing about in this book: the will to win, and the process through which that goal is realized.

It begins with a coach who, because he possesses a consuming passion for excellence and winning, communicates in his every word and deed a total commitment to those values. He "molds character" by expecting and demanding a similar level of commitment from his players, and by gradually weeding out those who do not share his vision of greatness or the willingness to work hard enough to make it a reality.

When the process is complete—that is, when the malcontents and players who expected an easy ride to greatness are gone—the coach is left with a small army of highly motivated, totally dedicated athletes who will give their all for him, for each other, and for the team. It is precisely at that point—and only then—that impossible dreams no longer seem impossible.

The material that follows has, in some cases, already been covered in the text. My intention in repeating it here is to place it in its proper context, namely, that of an overall program for success in coaching. These ten points are, in my estimation, the most important keys to success in coaching. They are not isolated factors like items on a shopping list; they are interrelated, and must be taken as a whole to be fully effective.

1. HAVE A DREAM

In coaching, as in life, things never seem to go as we expect them to. Sometimes we accomplish more than we set out to do, while at other times we fall short of our expectations. While the unexpected nature of events is what gives life its flavor and spice, it also brings its share of disappointment and dissatisfaction along the way.

Your dream of great achievement is what will sustain you in times of hardship and difficulty. It is the beacon that will guide you safely through, only slightly the worse for wear, whatever unexpected storms and turbulence arise in the daily execution of your coaching tasks—but only if you keep your eye on the beacon!

Your dream is the sum total of all of your hopes and expectations for success in coaching. It need not be a realistic dream—after all, could Coach John Wooden ever have imagined in his wildest dreams that he would someday win ten NCAA basketball championships at UCLA in the span of 12 years?

All that is necessary at this point is that you have a dream, an unquenchable desire to follow that dream wherever it may lead you, and an equally relentless willingness to work as long and as hard as necessary to fulfill your dream.*

---

*"If one advances confidently in the direction of his dreams, and endeavors to live the life he has imagined, he will meet with a success unexpected in common hours."—Henry David Thoreau

2. DON'T LET TEMPORARY SETBACKS DETER YOU

Don't let setbacks destroy your dream. To paraphrase an old saying, "the road to failure is paved with good intentions."

In coaching, everyone starts out with the best of intentions, and with initially high hopes and expectations for a long and successful career, with wins stockpiling themselves like missiles in a U.S. military arsenal. For many coaches, though, such dreams are actually daydreams; fantasies that they have no intention of turning into reality. Other coaches never bother to dream impossible dreams. Still others find that, for any of a variety of reasons, the dream isn't worth the effort involved in its pursuit, so they modify their ambitions downward.

Thus, we are left with a relatively small minority of coaches who possess both a dream of greatness and an utter unwillingness to compromise that dream in the face of what they see as merely temporary setbacks along the way. They will adjust to situations as necessary, but not to the extent of giving up on their dream or scaling it down to a more modest, "realistic" level.[†] And they will *win*.

They will win because they absolutely refuse to give in to the many temptations to accept less. They will win consistently because, wherever they go and whomever they coach, they will carry with missionary zeal the message that dreams *can* come true, and that mountains *can* be moved by those who believe.

You can be such a coach. But first you need the dream and the willingness to share your vision of greatness with the youngsters around you who are looking for just such a star to follow. They're there, all around you, young people who want and need meaning, direction, and purpose in

---

[†]This is not to say that your day-to-day, short-term goals should not be narrow, or realistic; they should. But you will accomplish far more in your entire coaching career than you will accomplish today, so it stands to reason that today's successes or failures should not define the limits of your dream.

their lives of the sort that your dream can provide. Your task is to find them and show them the way.

3. WORK HARDER TO ACHIEVE MORE

To achieve more than other people, work harder than they're working. The head coach, by virtue of his own work habits, sets the level of effort expected of everyone associated with the team. If the head coach is laid-back and superficial in his work habits and preparations, his players and assistants are not likely to feel any great compulsion to work harder than he does. He will not command their respect as a coach unless his dedication, perseverance, discipline, and leadership are such that they inspire those under him to work to the fullest measure of their ability on the team's behalf.

If, however, the coach is a tireless worker on the team's behalf, his players and assistant coaches likely will understand and accept their roles in achieving the objectives he has outlined for the team's eventual success, no matter how long or how difficult their tasks may be. But the process begins and ends with the head coach who communicates his dreams of greatness to his players and assistants, together with his expectations for how success is to be achieved; and who, by virtue of his unswerving devotion to the team and willingness to pay the price of success in terms of hard work, is able to inspire his players and assistant coaches to devote themselves wholeheartedly to pursuing his vision of greatness on the team's behalf.

Just as we should expect our players to give a total effort at all times, it follows that they have an equally valid right to expect the same from us.

This does not mean, of course, that we must run wind sprints or work out with our players (unless we want to) in order to show the extent of our dedication: while players' efforts are both physical and mental, our work as coaches is mostly mental, and is revealed by the extent of our preparation, organization, and continuing search for new and better ways to teach skills or adapt offensive or defensive playing styles to the abilities of our players. If we prepare and follow daily practice schedules; if we provide our players with detailed scouting reports, analyses of our next opponent's playing styles and strategies, and game plans outlining our own strategy for dealing with that opponent; and if we constantly attempt to identify and correct in practice those areas of weakness that affect our team's play, our players will accept that we are, in fact, working to the best of our ability on the team's behalf.

Our players likely already know this, of course, just as teachers know whether their principal is doing his best to provide students with a suitable learning environment and a quality education. Still, it doesn't hurt for us to point out to our players every now and then that, for example, we stayed up until two o'clock last night making adjustments in our defense that we think will improve the team's overall defensive play.

The reader will note that no mention has been made here of *winning*: while winning obviously is desirable, it does not always necessarily reflect the winning coach's work ethic. Sometimes winning occurs because one team simply has an abundance of superior athletes.

The best guide to evaluating our own work ethic is likely to be found in the extent to which our preparation (for example, game plans) consistently offers our teams their best chance of winning games, or at least of controlling opponents most of the time in areas of the game in which they normally excel. As is equally true in evaluating the work habits of other coaches, it is a matter of honestly and objectively deciding whether we have used our available talent to the fullest extent possible, win or lose.

To use an obvious example, if the opponents run out of gas in the latter stages of a game, it should be rather evident that their coach did not adequately prepare his team to play. In that regard, the second-worst feeling in coaching is when you lose to a team that was not adequately prepared or coached to win the game but won anyway, simply because they had superior talent.

The *worst* feeling in coaching is when you lose because you know in your heart that your team was not adequately prepared or coached to win.

4. DON'T BLAME OTHERS

Accept full responsibility within your coaching situation. Don't blame others, and don't expect anyone else to solve your problems for you. This process begins the moment we take on the responsibilities of our new job.

If, for example, we have just assumed a coaching position in a losing situation, we could blame the athletes, the student body, the community, the previous coach, or even all four, for the sorry state the program is in—but what good would it do? Complaining about the lack of superior athletes isn't going to teach the athletes on hand how to win. Anyway, nobody held a gun to our head and forced us to sign that contract.

Accepting full responsibility means taking charge and overseeing progress in every aspect of our program. If our feeder system is lacking, we should take positive steps to improve it, rather than just wishing it were better. If our booster club is sagging, we should search for ways to boost enrollment and revitalize the membership, starting with our own enthusiasm and willingness to work to make it better. If faculty involvement and interest in our program is low, we should find ways to get the teachers involved and reward their involvement. (One tried-and-true method of fostering positive teacher attitudes toward our program is to show an interest in, and support for, *their* areas of extracurricular involvement.)

5. SURROUND YOURSELF WITH GOOD PEOPLE

In a losing situation, attracting and retaining loyal supporters—especially athletes—who believe wholeheartedly in you and your program may be a discouragingly slow and tedious process; after all, why should players offer their wholehearted support for a program that is already in a shambles? Still, as you find ways to retain those players who accept you, your philosophy, your discipline, and your coaching methods, and to rid your program of those players who oppose you in your efforts to make changes where needed, your base of support will gradually broaden. (If it doesn't, you may, like the family in the movie *The Amityville Horror*, want to listen more closely to that unseen, whispering voice telling you to "Getttt Outtttt!")

6. CONCENTRATE ON PRIORITIES

Identify and concentrate your efforts on essential aspects of your coaching. Organize your life in terms of priorities, and stick to them. If you aren't careful, you can waste an incredible amount of time on nonessential tasks. As you probably know, the demands on a coach's time are many and varied, especially if he pursues his craft with his whole being. The end of one game marks the beginning of preparation for the next game, and so it goes, on and on. The successful coaches and their families understand this and learn to live with it, but it never gets any easier. In coaching, you're only as good as your last win, and the more you win, the more you're expected to win. The pressure to excel, and to *win*, never goes away, not entirely. Even as you read this, the next challenge to your dedication, perseverance, and problem-solving ability is no farther away than your telephone receiver.

The pressure and demands on your time are here to stay, at least, for as long as you remain in coaching. If you accept that fact, you may as well make the best of it by organizing your life and your coaching in terms of priorities. What sort of priorities?

Well, for starters, there's your family. If you're married, an understanding, supportive spouse is vital to your personal and professional well-being. It's lonely at the top, they say, but having someone to share the view with is awfully fulfilling, despite the struggles and frustrations encountered along the way.

If you're a college coach, recruiting had better rank among your top priorities. At worst, recruiting can be a vicious, dog-eat-dog world of cheating, downgrading the worth of other coaches and/or colleges, and using high-pressure intimidation tactics to lure immature young people into making spur-of-the-moment decisions that they'll later regret. At best, recruiting is virtually like holding down a second full-time job. The day is long past when coaches could, as John Wooden did, expect high school prospects to write them expressing an interest in attending their schools.

Other priorities and demands on your time include: working with players' problems (or problem players); running daily practices; scouting; devising game plans; keeping abreast of trends and changes in your sport; scheduling; teaching skills; working in summer camps; teaching a full load of classes; preparing daily lesson plans for each class period; conducting weekly television and/or radio shows; attending booster club meetings; ordering equipment and supplies; maintaining and/or supervising the playing field or gym; filling out requisitions, travel and expense vouchers, and eligibility reports; keeping a homeroom and attendance register, and so forth. Such a list barely scratches the surface of all the duties and responsibilities that demand a coach's time and attention. For instance, we've said nothing about the "free" time a coach spends searching for, and then adapting or refining, techniques, plays, patterns, or systems of offensive and defensive play that are suitable to his or her players' skills and level of ability.

Every coach should take time to sit down and list the priorities in his life in order to identify and concentrate his efforts on the most essential tasks at hand. Such an undertaking will never be wasted, since the result will be more efficient use of his valuable coaching time and increased understanding of what he expects and is willing to accomplish in his coaching.

7. SET REALISTIC GOALS

Set high, but realistic, goals—both short- and long-range—for yourself, your individual players, and your team. Look for and identify progress toward those goals. A vast difference exists between our dreams and our goals. Our dreams are the idyllic, fancied visions of greatness, or great accomplishment, that we bring with us to our work and that will nurture and sustain us through bad times. Our dreams are the sum total of all that we would like to accomplish in the best of all possible worlds, and not merely what we expect to accomplish, whether today or in our coaching careers.

Our goals, whether short- or long-range, are the daily blueprints and master plans we devise and follow in our day-to-day pursuit of those nebulous dreams. The more carefully we define, evaluate, and revise those goals as necessary, the more likely we are to achieve them. This is, in fact, a major component of the process of becoming (or remaining) a consistent winner.

When we spoke of hard work in Point 3 previously, we were addressing precisely this aspect of coaching; namely, the amount of time a coach is ready, willing and able to devote to devising appropriate goals, both short- and long-range, for himself, his team, and the individual players; evaluating progress toward accomplishing those goals; and revising the goals either upward or downward as often as necessary—that is, upward revision to provide continued challenge as goals are accomplished, or downward revision when goals have been set too high and failure to reach them may have a detrimental effect on morale.

Another way of putting it is, the more often our daily actions are directed toward achieving our coaching goals, the more likely we are to achieve those goals, and to achieve them sooner.

We can look to divine providence or luck to provide us with solutions to our coaching problems, but until we accept the necessity of adopting goal-oriented behavior; that is, pursuing the goals we have set and coming to grips with our problems in a logical, ordered manner and on a continuing basis, we cannot realistically expect to find viable solutions to our coaching problems more often than occasionally.

We are the best solution to our coaching problems. If we can remember that fact and apply it to every aspect of our coaching, we may not have to complain, as did one of the characters in Walt Kelly's comic strip "Pogo," "We have met the enemy, and he is us."

8. DON'T UNDERESTIMATE YOURSELF

Don't limit yourself or your potential for success in coaching. And conversely, don't expect more from your coaching than you are willing to put into it. You don't have to be a genius to be a great coach, but you *do* need to understand the elements involved in getting where you want to go. Bear Bryant used to love to tell people that he was just a dumb country boy who was smart enough to hire brilliant assistant coaches who made him look good. He wasn't dumb, of course, not by a long shot—but his statement illustrates my point: if you apply yourself rigorously to every aspect of your coaching, you'll want to identify those elements that are necessary to achieve success, and then work to the fullest extent possible to master them.

The danger here is that you may fall prey to the belief that success can be achieved with less than your best efforts. This is especially true if your present coaching situation is such that every time someone shakes a tree, seven or eight more superior athletes fall out.

When you aren't blessed with superior athletes on your

teams, the best way to make up the difference is to outwork other coaches who *do* have superior athletes.

When you do have superior athletes, though, you still must work hard to stay ahead of them and endeavor to find a style of play that emphasizes and uses their considerable skills to the fullest extent possible.

9. INSTILL DISCIPLINE IN YOUR TEAMS

Reduced to its lowest common denominator, the coaching task involves attracting potentially talented players into one's program, and then teaching them to perform the skills associated with that sport. Obviously, the better a coach is at either or both of those activities, the more successful he will be in his coaching.

Discipline and motivation are the keys to controlling the outcome of teaching and learning situations. Players must be motivated to concentrate and perform with intensity, and they must recognize the necessity of discipline in their lives.

In the best of all possible worlds, players would do whatever they wanted to do, whenever and wherever they wanted to do it, and the results would be satisfactory to all concerned. But ours is an imperfect world, and athletes in team sports cannot be left to their own devices, especially regarding their training and development. Even the most dedicated of athletes in team sports would slack off in their performances in practice or in games without the presence of a coach or coaches to direct their efforts. I believe this, as I'm sure you do, too.

From a coaching standpoint, discipline is more than punishment or using the threat of punishment to impose one's will on individuals or the team. It also refers to any sort of behavior or training on the coach's part that is intended to develop self-control, orderliness, efficiency, or other desirable behavior in his players. Coaches vary widely in the amount of control, or discipline, that they feel is necessary to exercise over their teams and players; best advice here is to err on the side of strict discipline. For one thing, young people need discipline in their lives; for another, learning is so vital to team and player development that it cannot be left to chance: the learning environment must be controlled through strict discipline. The alternatives to discipline are chaos and confusion.

10. BUILD A SENSE OF "TEAMNESS" IN EVERYTHING YOU DO

In the estimation of many philosophers, the meaning of life is to be found in the act of committing oneself and one's efforts totally toward the achievement of a higher purpose than oneself. And in team sports, The Team is that higher purpose. The more closely knit the team, the harder its individual members will pull together to achieve team goals, and the more lasting will the rewards of victory be felt.

FINAL THOUGHTS ON WINNING BIG

chapter **9**

My ambition is to win more than anybody
else. It makes you feel good to know you've
accomplished what no one else has.

—*Jack Nicklaus*

In reading the original finished manuscript of this book, I realized that I had inadvertently omitted three of the most important points concerning making a winning career in coaching. These three points, taken together because they cannot possibly be separated, have enabled some coaches— the best ones in the profession—to build incredible winning records that literally span decades of successful coaching.

1. YOU HAVE TO LOVE COACHING

As my father-in-law, the late Joe Bell, himself a highly successful high school basketball, track, and baseball coach, put it, "If you can live without coaching, don't get into it." On a per-hour basis, virtually everyone in our society who works at all makes more money than the average coach, and with infinitely fewer hassles along the way. I can't imagine a tougher job than coaching, especially if you're trying to make ends meet and raise a family too. If you don't have a deep-seated love for coaching, you won't last in the profession. And to make it worse, neither I nor anyone else can supply you with adequate reasons for staying in coaching. You'll have to find them for yourself.

2. YOU HAVE TO STAY IN COACHING

By punching in a few numbers on the old calculator, it should be rather easy to show that if your goal is to win, say, 200 football games in your coaching career, you'd better plan to remain in the profession for at least a couple of decades. (Or else you'd better find a way to play 20 to 30 football games a year to make up the difference.) For example, of the 15 men who have ever won 200 or more football games in the Georgia High School Association, the *least* number of years coached by any of them is 22.

Assuming that you're a good enough coach to avoid being driven out of the profession by an annoying inability to win occasionally, the most likely threats to your coaching longevity are financial considerations, especially when a family is involved; the inordinate amount of time spent away from home or traveling; the pressures to win (which, over a number of years, can produce ulcers, high blood pressure, and a variety of other nervous disorders that adversely affect one's physical and mental health); and a loss of enthusiasm with coaching, teaching, or a combination of the two, which can be brought on or made worse by any of the previous factors.

3. YOU HAVE TO FIND THE RIGHT SCHOOL

As one veteran coach put it, "If you're happy where you are, you'll stay there; if not, you'll go somewhere else. And if you go to three or four places and don't like any of them, you'll probably decide that it's the *coaching* that's making you unhappy rather than the schools. And you'll drop quietly out of coaching."

If, however, you stay in one school long enough to build a highly successful program, you're likely to remain there long after your building phase is complete in order to reap the harvest of wins that you earned while paying your coaching dues. After you've been at the same school for a number of years and established a winning tradition, winning comes easier and easier. The community gets behind your teams, and parents and students apply pressure on your players to keep the winning tradition going. Every year the players want their team to be at least as good, and preferably better, than last year's team; they don't want to be known as the team that let the community down.

The key here is that you must be honest with yourself. After settling into a new coaching situation, you'll know whether you realistically have a chance of building the kind of program at that school that you want to build. If not, you should plan accordingly. And if so, well, the sky's the limit. *You can accomplish whatever you set out to accomplish in coaching*—provided, that is, that you love coaching enough to stay in it until you find the school and the coaching situation that is right for you.

As another coach put it, "If you're gonna stay in coaching as long as I have, it helps to be crazy—either crazy about your sport, or just plain crazy!"

INDEX